YOU ARE
AWESOME!

Eight Practices to Unleash
Your Extraordinary Self

Sebastian King

BALBOA
PRESS

A DIVISION OF HAY HOUSE

Balboa Press books may be ordered through booksellers or by contacting:

Balboa Press
A Division of Hay House
1663 Liberty Drive
Bloomington, IN 47403
www.balboapress.com.au
1 (877) 407-4847

Print information available on the last page.

ISBN: 978-1-5043-0337-8 (sc)
ISBN: 978-1-5043-0338-5 (e)

Balboa Press rev. date: 07/04/2016

Contents

Acknowledgements

I would like to acknowledge many people who have supported me and inspired me. First of all, I thank my wife, Libby Ellis. I also want to thank my former business coach, Kerry Grace, and all my other friends and family who have helped me get this book completed.

This book, thoughts, and ideas within it have been inspired by the wisdom in the teachings of Buddhism, Christianity, Hinduism, Judaism, and other spiritual paths. I have also found inspiration from many wonderful lecturers, theorists, spiritualists, writers, and speakers. Some of these, in no particular order, are Laura and Fritz Perls, the many teachers and lecturers associated with the Sydney Gestalt Institute, Louise Hay, Cheryl Richardson, Neale Donald Walsch, Wayne Dyer, Robert Holden, Eckhart Tolle, Robert Lee, Gordon Wheeler and many other Gestalt authors, the teachings of Buddha, the teachings of Jesus, the teachings of the Tao, Plato, Aristotle, Bell Hooks, Jean Paul Sartre, William Shakespeare, Virginia Woolf, Deepak Chopra, His Holiness the Dalai Lama, Ven. Jetsunma Tenzin Palmo, Victor Frankl, Satya Narayan Goenka, Christopher

Titmuss, Abraham Maslow, Brene Brown, Martin Buber, and Sri Nisargadatta Maharaj.

I am, of course, probably missing some people in this list, and my apologies to you.

With love and gratitude, I thank all the people who have sparked ideas in me and given me guidance through their words, actions, kindnesses, and love.

Chapter 1

Tragedy to Transformation

Knowing others is intelligence;
Knowing yourself is true wisdom.
—Lao-tzu[1]

Did you know that you are already awesome?

How is that? I know that you are awesome because you bought my book! Thank you; this helps to pay the bills.

You didn't know that you were awesome? Well, let's get to work then. But before that, let me start by telling you a bit of a story.

I would like you to imagine yourself in the following scenario. You are in your early twenties. It is the end of summer, and you are about to return to university. You and one of your best friends decide to go on a great road trip from where you live (in Ontario, Canada) all the way to Tofino in British Columbia (on the other side of Canada). This is an ambitious road trip, totalling nearly nine thousand kilometres.

It is the end of this journey, and the two of you are returning home for the final few days of the last long weekend of summer. You are behind the wheel of the car with only about eight hours to go. You and your friend have an unopened case of beer in the back. You are both looking forward to seeing your mutual friends and sharing your experiences with them when you arrive.

Then you see it. A car is coming toward you, and it is spinning into your lane.

Everything suddenly seems to slow down. You see a drop-off to one side of the car and a rock wall on the other. You swear out loud; all the while your foot is on the brake. Then, with an enormous crash, your whole world changes.

Everything goes dark and blank.

You wake up in a daze and realise that your life has been forever impacted. You have been in a massive car accident. Your right knee is mangled. Your right thighbone is at an unnatural angle. There is glass everywhere. The steering wheel is much closer to you than it was before. Your friend appears to be cut and wide-eyed as well.

You then notice many people around the car. Soon after, the pain and anxiety start to set in. You look out of where the window used to be and see the car that smashed into you. You see a blanket draped over the driver's side, and you know the person who was in that car must be dead, although no one assisting you would say so. You have no sense of time except the timelessness that occurs with the agony and horror of looking at your leg and knee. Apparently it takes them close to an hour to get you out of the car, into the ambulance, and on the way to a hospital.

After being driven to one hospital and then flown to another because of the nature of your injuries, you come awake to discover that there are tubes attached to you. You learn that you have been in surgery for a full day. You feel excruciating pain and crushing anxiety. You do not want to be where you are, but no one seems to be listening to you.

After a while your parents arrive. You still do not fully understand what has happened to you. After a few hours of suffering and on-again/off-again sleep, you blank out again. The next thing you know, you come to in a haze. They tell you that you have been on life support for three full weeks, but they brought you out because you are getting better. You then find out you had to be flown to yet another hospital in Toronto, one that provides care and treatment for you that the previous hospital could not provide. Your parents and brother are there with you, and you see they are simultaneously relieved and concerned for you.

You are then informed that you are lucky to have survived and that you had a fat embolism in your lungs that caused them to stop working completely. You learn that your parents, brother, and best friend were told at one point that you would not make it through the night. In other words, they were told to prepare for your death.

When you were on life support, you were apparently communicating with people, but you have absolutely no memories of this at all. You don't remember the many loving and concerned visitors who saw you while you were in intensive care. All you can remember are visions or hallucinations that are still vivid to you to this very day. After being taken off life support, you are moved to yet another hospital and yet *another* after that, making it five hospitals that you have been to since the car accident.

You then have to learn how to walk again. Your muscles have been damaged and have become a bit atrophied. After all this, you need to learn to confront a newfound fear of cars and driving.

You also need to learn how to take in and accept an outpouring of love and care from everyone around you, as well as from people you were not necessarily close to before your accident. And all the while, you are trying to deal with a post-traumatic stress disorder brought on by your experiences. Then you undergo a few more surgeries on your knee as the years go by.

This is my story. I was in a car accident where a driver who had a couple of drinks hit the car I was driving. This accident almost took my life. It also created a personal trauma for myself and for my good friend and caused much distress for my family and circles of friends.

This was also one of the biggest turning points in my life, and it created a new focus for me. Some of these changes were quick; others took me a number of years to learn, absorb, and appreciate. In some ways, I am still learning the lessons of that experience. In fact, I find I am often learning new lessons from not just the accident but from many of my other life changes as well, both the ones I have labelled as good and the ones I have labelled as bad.

These experiences have taught me to learn how to accept myself for who I am. I have also learned a great deal about what love is. Eventually, I also discovered how awesome and extraordinary my life really is. Finally, I discovered that there is a fire burning in me that compels me to share my story and what I have learned with you.

I can also see that as horrible as this experience sounds (and it was pretty horrible at the time, I can tell you), it has also become an awesome experience for me. Not in the way of getting attention by bragging about it to gain sympathy (something I did for many years) but, rather, in that it allows me to see the beauty in my life and all of life, for that matter. I can say in full confidence that the car accident that almost took my life has become an awesome experience for which I am grateful. It has helped me to grow and become the person I am today.

More of My Story

As it is with each of us, my life experiences have informed who I am. They have also contributed to the insights I will be sharing with you. Like you, I have had my ups and downs, my joys and grief, and my happiness and frustrations. Like you, I have had an awesome life, although it took me a long time to realise that. To be truthful, I still need to remind myself of this when I am feeling stress or anxiety.

I grew up in a small town called Gravenhurst in Ontario, Canada. It is a beautiful area surrounded by forests and lakes. My parents are wonderful people who raised me to respect others and the environment around me. They also instilled in me an adventurous spirit and a desire to experience the new, a mindset that has taken me around the world. When I wrote this book, I was living with my beautiful wife in the Blue Mountains in Australia, an area that is surrounded by lush landscapes. We ended up there as a result of travelling and our desire to experience new things.

I went to the only high school in my town, aptly called Gravenhurst High School. My upbringing was filled with its own joys, losses, celebrations, and traumas. With a few exceptions, it was not really that different from what most of the other kids I grew up with experienced. I am still in touch with a number of friends I had when I was a child, and this is something for which I am truly grateful. Like all young people, I made mistakes, and this sometimes caused hurt to people. My actions during this period created guilt within me that I had not been able to assuage until more recently in my life. However, I also had many good experiences and still hold many cherished memories of when I was younger.

After high school, I went on a three-and-a-half-month trip through Europe with my girlfriend at the time. It was an eye-opening and awesome experience for me that was filled with adventure, arrogance, and hubris. I sometimes shake my head ruefully at what I did at that time of my life. We lived off of fruit, cheese, cold cuts, and baguettes that would get so hard after a day that they were like baseball or cricket bats. The many family trips with my parents sparked the travel bug within me. It was this first trip to Europe that really helped me start to see how different people can be throughout the world.

I attended York University where I attained an undergraduate degree in English Literature and Philosophy. University life was filled with parties, lots of reading, lots of parties, and lots and lots of essay writing, and, of course, lots of parties. I was double majoring in English Literature and Philosophy, after all. I spent my time in cafes, pubs, and clubs and enjoyed a lot of live music. Live music is still an awesome part of my life and an ongoing passion for me. I got involved in social and environmental activism around a variety of concerns, and this also taught me a lot about people and later, upon reflection, about myself as well.

In my late twenties, I went on an around the world trip, visited many countries, and had both wonderful and challenging experiences. At that time, I met the woman who would later become my wife in Australia through a mutual friend I went to university with. This led me to move to Australia, going to school again and receiving a Post-Graduate Degree in Gestalt Psychotherapy. My friend David married another wonderful Australian woman, and they live in Australia as well. Isn't that awesome and extraordinary?

I share this very small part of my personal story with you to outline how these experiences have influenced who I am. I also want to express that these regular, everyday experiences are also part of what make me awesome and create an extraordinary life for me. Through the sharing of some of my everyday experiences, I hope to assist you with learning that there is awesomeness in your life as well. Maybe you have not travelled like I have, but I am sure you have had similar life experiences of possibly working, finding or searching for love, going to school, hanging out with good friends, and so forth.

It has been through my experiences that I have arrived at the insights I want to share with you. My experiences—good, bad, painful, and joyous—come together to show me that I have awesomeness in my life, and I can access the beauty of love, gratitude, and compassion to allow this inner awesomeness to blossom and bloom into the extraordinary life I live today.

My first bit of advice is that I encourage everyone to try something new to them, such as I have done with writing this book. There are benefits and learning to be gained from having both good and poor experiences of new things. It has been an awesome and liberating feeling for me to express and experience myself in new ways, whether it has been through writing this book or through things like traveling to new places that have taken me out of my comfort zones. The experience of the new has assisted me in realising that there is an extraordinariness that exists within me and, in fact, within all people. This includes you.

Try new experiences, and see where they will take you. These journeys can be both external and internal. I say, give them a try, and see what happens.

The Book

How does one start a book? This is a question I have asked myself for years, or at least different versions of the same theme on beginning or starting the journey of writing. I have spent much time engaging in self-improvement, reading the teachings of many people I admire, and educating myself. All the while, I have often had thoughts of writing. Does this or something similar sound familiar to you? Have you ever had a recurring idea, thought, desire, or pull towards something that consistently keeps coming back? For me, this has been writing.

I have had thoughts of writing going as far back in my life as to my primary school years. Then one day near the end of 2012, I had a realisation that moved from my mind into my body and then into my spirit. In that moment, I not only had an intellectual understanding that my life has the potential for being awesome but a full knowing within all aspects of my being that this was so. Even more than that, I knew that every single one of us has that potential within us and, hence, a new starting point within my personal journey began, and that led to the writing of this book. It is so wonderful to me that I get to share with all of you the knowledge that you are awesome and extraordinary as well.

Throughout my life journey, I often wrote small pieces of my thoughts onto bits of paper, into diaries, and into my computer or mobile phone. I even remember sitting with a friend when we were about ten years old or so, writing out little bits of what I would now call philosophy or insights onto pieces of paper. At the time, my mother kept these and showed them to her friends. I wonder if she still has those bits of paper.

I have had many different thoughts, ideas, and inspirations along the way. Some of my ideas were for writing fiction, and yet others were philosophical or spiritual in nature. As part of my personal creative process, I have had many thoughts come together, and like drops of water, they sometimes coalesced into larger wholes. Sometimes they seemed to split off into what seemed to be separate thoughts or fragments, much like the spray from a waterfall. This book has been one of those coming together moments for me. A unity of thoughts and ideas coming together into a cohesive whole that makes sense to me and that I now want to share with you.

Through writing this book, I am continuing in my process of self-discovery, of exploring my inner awesomeness and the inner awesomeness of others.

You will be joining me in examining the personal insights I have discovered that have led me to this current part of my pathway. This book is a process of reviewing and revealing how I look at and move through the world. It is my hope that my thinking resonates with you on some level, whether it is in agreement, disagreement, or a bit of both. My purpose is to explore what I know that helps lead me to inner peace and inner harmony. One of the benefits of sharing this, I hope, is that you may examine your life and start to understand how you are awesome and extraordinary yourself.

I was passionate about writing this book, but before starting to write, I had some self-doubt and felt some of my own vulnerability. I was worried that other people had already said and written about what I wanted to say. What I realised, with the support of others—with a big shout out to my wife, Libby, and my former business coach, Kerry Grace—is that what I am doing is actually expressing my own experiences and thoughts, and gaining some personal learning through allowing myself to experience my own vulnerability. Yes, for me to write this book has been a process of entering into my own vulnerability, and I can honestly say this has been truly awesome for me. To find my own words and experience others' words and thoughts in a way that makes sense to me on my personal journey have been both enlightening and inspirational for me. This has been a truly humbling, empowering, and extraordinary gift. I have discovered that vulnerability is definitely something that can be awesome.

Another part of my experience of vulnerability that I want to share with you is also in relation to this book. I will come clean here and say that I sat on my manuscript for over a year. I was resistant to doing my final edit, even after arranging my publishing contract with Balboa Press. Even though I had written most of what you will read in this book, I was feeling blocked in finishing.

Not long ago, I was feeling a moodiness and anxiety that was permeating many parts of my life. This included feeling stressed over not finishing my final edits. When I started to think about these things, I contemplated how I have experienced anxiety many times in my life. This contemplation then led me to the realisation that I have never really acknowledged or spoken about how I have experienced anxiety as far back as I can remember.

In fact, I experience anxiety on a regular basis. One example of this is when I am at the point of entering into groups or crowds of people. When this happens, I feel my emotions rise and will often not want to be there. This will be a surprise to many people I know as I can be really quite social and engaging. What I have learned to do is free fall into these situations. I just go for it, and through experience, I have learned that I can sometimes lessen my anxiety through engaging with others.

I also learned at a younger age that alcohol can help me in party- or dinner-type situations as well, I know this is not healthy for me, and I have been doing much less of this for a while now. I had realised long ago that using alcohol in these types of situations did not always serve me well, even though I was not yet fully acknowledging my anxiety at that time.

These are examples of some coping mechanisms that have worked for me through the years. My recent insights are now showing me that some of my other coping strategies, clever as they have been, are currently not always in my own best interest for what I want to achieve in my life. Since I have had these insights and started to acknowledge and honour my anxiety, I have been able to seek support and reengage in finishing this book, among other things, which included, of course, adding this section.

I think it is awesome how through honouring my anxiety, I have been able to do all this. I will speak more on these processes later in the book. You see, even though I have learned much in the way of how to take action in my life, I still have to practice what I have learned in order to gain new personal insights. This is awesome as well as this reminds me that my emotional state and interpretations of my experiences are not static and can shift.

One thing that I want to make clear from the beginning of this book is that I am not promoting a therapy. What I am writing about is a system of tools that we can use to recognise how we can be awesome and extraordinary in all aspects of our lives. This is not meant as a replacement for sound counselling advice from trained and accredited counsellors, psychotherapists, psychologists, and psychiatrists.

I have been guided through difficult times by trained professionals who have assisted me with issues that were too difficult for me to sort through on my own. Actually, I still have a counsellor I see and greatly appreciate. I also have previous counsellors in my life I know I can still turn to if I have need of counselling and support through confusing or difficult times. By all means, if you feel you have something that needs to be addressed, seek assistance from a professional. If you have been recommended and or referred to an accredited professional and have started to seek support from him or her, continuing to follow professional guidance could be beneficial for you. Of course, stick with someone who works for you personally and with whom you are comfortable as this can help with any process you are engaged in. Even though I have been trained and practiced as a Psychotherapist, this book is not meant to replace the good work that is done by those good people.

To me, this book is about sharing with you my insights into how, no matter where any of us are at in our lives, we have the potential to be awesome. I am here to share with you how we can all be expressions of love and awesomeness in our lives.

Thank you for taking the time to participate in this journey with me. You are awesome even if you do not know it yet.

Some of the Awesomeness in My Life

Now I would like to share with you some of the awesomeness in my life.

The first bit of extraordinariness I want to share is the love and gratitude I send out to my family, my friends, and some wonderful people in the Canadian health care system who helped me to come through a near-death experience and enter into a healthy recovery process. This helped me to discover that my life is truly awesome and wonderful, and that I am surrounded by many people who love and care about me.

It is awesome that I have married a wonderful woman who is supportive and loving. She has also created her own business, running a social enterprise called InCharge that assists people with disabilities and their families. I like to think that her awesomeness also rubs off onto me.

I grew up in an awesome country, and I now live in another awesome country. All the wonderful travelling I have done has opened my eyes to the extraordinariness that exists all over the world. It was this wonderful experience of travel that led me to meeting my most awesome and extraordinary wife.

A few years ago I spent close to half a year in India doing addiction counselling for Tibetan refugees. This was an awesome experience that humbled me and let me use and develop my skills while also creating the circumstances for me to meet many great people. This still stands out as being a wonderfully awesome time for me. It is truly extraordinary to me that people in that community trusted me to work with them on such an emotional level. I want to send lots of big love out to Tenzin Woaber. I hope we meet again someday, my friend.

I have helped many cancer patients and carers through their cancer journeys and engaged the community at large on issues concerning cancer. This has taught me much about resilience, vulnerability, and love. I am grateful for these awe-inspiring opportunities.

I have many great friends to whom I can and have turned to for assistance. I have also been there for them when they needed my assistance, and both are truly awesome and wondrous things to me.

We live in a beautiful area surrounded by bush (or forest, for non-Australians) where we grow some of our own veggies. There is a wonderfully artistic community where we can socialize with like-minded people who are also awesome.

It is also awesome that I am skilled in assisting people through difficult times when they come to me for support.

The last bit of awesomeness that I would like to share with you is that it has been an amazingly wonderful experience to write this book and to be supported in doing so by many great people, including my wife, my friends, and my business coach. I can honestly say that I feel extraordinarily blessed.

Chapter 2

Let's Start Discovering
the Awesome

Awe

A feeling of reverential respect mixed with fear or wonder:[2]

> An emotion variously combining dread, veneration, and wonder that is inspired by authority or by the sacred or sublime[3]

Extraordinary

> Very unusual or remarkable: or, Unusually great:[4]

> Very different from what is normal or ordinary. Extremely good or impressive.[5]

Am I awesome? Is my life awesome? Are the people who surround me awesome? These are a few of the questions that

I have asked myself on my own journey through discovering the awesomeness in my life. As I have explored questions like this for myself, I have come to many realisations about who I am and how I perceive the world. This has led me on a personal journey where I have been learning to love myself, learning to respect myself, and learning to be grateful for what is in my life. All of which has taught me that I have the potential within me to be extraordinary.

"Awesome" is a bit of a funny word to me. For a few years now I have been hearing it used more and more as an expression of joy and happiness, as a description of memorable events, and as a way of framing relationships between people. I remember a few years ago using the word but also seeing it as something that is a bit cheesy and kind of funny, if you know what I mean. For a while I was a bit of a wanker about it and thought that it should only be used in certain contexts—the awesome fool that I was. More recently, I started to think more about the word and realised just how wonderful and apt it is for describing and expressing the feelings I have.

As the definitions above imply for the root word of "awe," it is something that can be used to express a mixed variety of experiences that are significant. I have realised that when I use the word "awesome," I can create a new framework for myself that assists me in honouring all my experiences and emotions. So when I use this word and say to myself that I am awesome, I can experience a feeling of wholeness within myself that can also extend to those around me.

What does it mean to be extraordinary? Can I be extraordinary? These are also a few more questions I have asked myself. Through having experiences that I have labelled as either good or bad and reflecting on them through the lens of some of the lessons I share in this book, I have come to realise that I have an extraordinary life. I have learned that when I choose to believe and act as though my life is extraordinary, extraordinary things happen for me.

I do not want to turn the idea of extraordinary into something that becomes ordinary. Rather, from my perspective, I am putting forward the idea that we all use the idea of having the potential to be extraordinary as a way for us to be personally inspired, to motivate us, and to create self-definitions that can be beneficial to us. When you get right down to it, it does not matter if others feel you are extraordinary; rather, it is about how you feel about yourself.

When I feel extraordinary about myself from an inner place of peace not based on an ego and where I see others as less than, and I am able at the same time to not be emotionally attached to my preconceived beliefs about the outcomes of my actions, awesome things can happen for me.

Before I go any further, you are probably reading this because something about the words "awesome" or "extraordinary" resonates with you or makes you curious. The way I have written the book is that there are interactive parts. I will pose questions for you to think about or answer as we go along. So I would like to start that process with you now before continuing.

Being Awesome

I want to begin with asking you three questions about you and awesomeness. These are meant to begin to assist you with the understanding of the eight practices I present. If you want, take a few moments to clear your head, and take a few breaths and get grounded. There are no right or wrong answers, so anything that comes up is, as the expression goes, the bee's knees. Feel free to expand on your answers.

Is my life awesome?

Could my life have more awesomeness in it?

Am I willing to step into being awesome?

Learning the Path of Awesomeness

What stops us from being awesome? What prevents us from having the lives that we want to have? What is it that gets in our way? We can all come up with many reasons for why we do not achieve what we want to achieve. There are many things that we believe get in our way and stop us from doing what we want to do. Sometimes we believe it is our situation, our job, our partners, our workmates, our friends; the list can go on and on for as many people as there are in the world. I have learned that usually the most limiting factors that we experience are the ones we have within ourselves. The attitudes, behaviours, and judgements that we have chosen, learned, or adopted in our lives are often what create the barriers we perceive. These are the things that I have seen get in my way of realising I can have an extraordinary and awesome life.

I have learned the challenges we face in life are opportunities to learn more about ourselves and the world around us. They can be opportunities to come into healthier relationships with others, to learn to love more fully, and to get more in tune with Source or God or the Universe, depending on how you perceive the world we live in. But at the same time, it can be a difficult thing to engage with these lessons as we are emotional beings with a variety of responses and experiences that we have gained throughout our lives.

Sometimes we can feel overwhelmed in our responses to certain situations. This can be confusing and even debilitating at times. It is sometimes difficult to see what may feel like wounding or hurtful situations as opportunities. When your partner cheats on you, if you have been physically hurt by someone, or you have had a loved one die, it can be difficult to see opportunities for our lives. To me, part of the key for shifting my thinking in these types of situations is learning to let love exist in my heart more and to honour the emotions that have arisen in each of the types of situations as they arise. Sometimes I can do this right away, and other times it is through reflection that I start to feel my personal shifts.

I do understand and can see how circumstances can definitely play a role in inhibiting us on our paths to experiencing awesomeness. In fact, I can think of many examples where very difficult circumstances beyond people's control make it difficult to even contemplate these pathways. Maslow's

Hierarchy of Needs[6] comes to mind, and if someone is in a situation where, for instance, one's physiological or safety needs are not being met or are a struggle to meet, shifting emotional or intellectual mindsets around things can be exceptionally difficult.

I would, however, also argue that for a lot of people, myself most definitely included at the top of the list, circumstances do not need to be the ultimate deal-breaker we often make them out to be. I have learned that sometimes I really just need to learn how to navigate these difficult circumstances with new and different thinking to discover my own awesomeness. When I am able to navigate through difficult times, I know I am on the path of leading an extraordinary life.

We all want to be happy in our lives, to be satisfied, and to be content in what we do. But what is it that really stops us, assuming our basic needs are being met? The answer is simple, yet it feels so complex to a lot of people. I know it used to feel complex to me, and, in fact, sometimes those old thinking patterns still do come up. The answer is so simple that it is often rejected as hubris or ego. The answer lies within all of us. The answer is that *we* are what can stop us. But we are also that which can move us beyond what we perceive as barriers or blockages. To quote some old aphorisms, "We are our own worst enemy," but we are also, "Our own best friend."

Introducing the Eight Practices

I would now like to share with you a brief description of each of the eight practices I explore in the rest of the book. These are short descriptions outlining some of the thoughts I have had around the following concepts: developing awareness of the present moment, rethinking my repetitive behaviours, honouring my emotions, developing relationships, learning to love more, engaging in celebration, and lastly, learning to forgive.

1. By living from the present moment and developing my personal awareness, I discover and live in my personal power.

In this chapter I explore how through developing our awareness we are better able to live from the present moment and create awesomeness in our lives. I look at how if we live too much in either the past or the future, we can create unhelpful patterns in our lives that do not serve the vision of who we want to be.

2. Through reframing my repetitive behaviours, I can nurture my wisdom and fuel my creativity.

I look at how through using our awareness, we can start to recognise the repetitive behaviours that no longer serve us. When we start to recognise unhelpful behaviours, we begin to observe how they no longer serve us. When this begins to occur, we can start to think about them in new and different ways. This can assist us in creating awesomeness in our lives.

I explore how behaviours we have that we see as "bad habits" can start to be seen as wise and creative choices that were made given the circumstances we have experienced in our lives. Our behaviours can then become signposts in our lives that we can choose to learn from. They provide us with personal lessons and help us to understand how we can be the person we want to be. So when we look at our how we have crafted our repetitive behaviours, we can start to realise that we were actually being quite extraordinary at the time they were created.

3. When I honour and respect all of my emotions, I can learn to shift the ones that hold me in unhelpful and repetitive patterns.

I explore how through learning to honour all our emotions, we are also learning how to experience the full range of who we are. As we practice this, we acquire skills that assist us with shifting away from the shame processes that can inhibit us. As we become aware of these processes, we can start to understand our behaviours in a new and different way. Our shame then starts to lose its meaning, and this opens a new way of thinking about our emotions that can lead to more awesome experiences for us. These new personal processes can assist us to see how we can make different choices in our lives that are more in alignment with who we want to be, thus leading us into having extraordinary lives.

4. Change can also occur through developing awesome relationships.

In this section, I explore how change can occur through developing a relationship with ourselves, with others, and with our communities at large. I look at how when we start to develop a relationship with ourselves, we create the opportunity to learn to take care of our physical, emotional, and spiritual well-being. Also, as we learn to nurture healthy relationships with others, we start to attract more of these supportive relationships into our lives. Then, through developing relationships within communities, we see how great things can be accomplished that are difficult to do alone.

5. As I learn how to feel and express love in new and different ways, I also learn how love assists me in creating an awesome and extraordinary ongoing experience of contentment, clarity, and fulfilment.

In this chapter I look at how as we start to refine—or in some cases even to acquire the skills of how to truly love ourselves, how to love others unconditionally, and how to express our love to all things—we can discover a personal fullness in our lives that makes us realise that we, too, can be awesome.

When we nurture our self-love, we feel more relaxed and peaceful, and this makes it easier for us to make the healthy and productive choices that we want to make for ourselves.

Through expressing love to others and feeling love from them, we feel a heightened sense of connection that provides us with the opportunity to learn more about ourselves. Then, through expressing our love to all things, we learn that we have a connection to all things, and it is this love that creates these connections. All of these expressions of love assist us in seeing how we can attract things into our lives that are positive and in alignment with how we want to live.

6. Engaging in celebration honours achievements, opens up the opportunity for further creativity, and cultivates community.

In this chapter I look at how when we engage in celebrations, we cultivate relationships and communities and honour our own achievements and those of others. These things can be an awesome way of capturing and expressing our creativity.

Celebration is important as it connects us to what we have achieved. It can also provide us with opportunities to connect with others and what they have accomplished in their lives. Through honouring our achievements, we express self-love. Through honouring other people's achievements, we are also given an opportunity to share love with others.

Celebration also provides us with the circumstances for not only honouring creativity but also a way of expressing it at the same time.

When we are celebrating, we are expressing the personal power we derive from acknowledging and living from the present moment.

7. I have learned and experienced how forgiveness can set me free.

Throughout this part, I share how through having my own experience of learning to forgive others, I have seen that forgiveness is like a balm that only I can apply to myself. Forgiveness to myself from myself is also a part of this process. I have learned that we can be our own worst enemy in the forgiveness process. When we learn to accept the past as the past and learn from it, we can free ourselves of repetitive thoughts and emotions in the present that may not be serving us. When we have done this, we can then start connecting with others and share the self-love that arises within us as we let go of those things that bind us.

8. I have learned that gratitude is an active process of accepting, appreciating, and acknowledging the abundant love that exists in others and myself.

Gratitude is a process that allows me to connect to my inner love, to express my personal power, and to nurture the relationships in my life. I have observed within others and myself that when we practice gratitude a few things can occur. I have seen that being grateful in the present moment can bring on a sense of peacefulness. When someone expresses gratitude towards me for something I have done, this can also lift my spirits and make me feel better. In close relationships, gratitude is also a way for me to connect my love with the love that exists in others and bring us closer.

Some Exercises on Awesomeness for You

Before we move onto exploring the eight practices in more depth, I would like you to answer these questions. I will ask you to write three examples for each, but you can do as few or as many as you like. If you really want to challenge yourself, try writing up to ten or more for each.

Please write down three awesome things about yourself.

Please write down three awesome things about relationships in your life.

Please write down three awesome things about your community.

Please write down three things you would like to be more awesome in your life.

Chapter 3

The Present Moment

Is My Place of Personal Power

By living from the present moment and developing my personal awareness, I discover and live in my personal power.

In this chapter I explore how in developing our awareness, we are better able to live from the present moment and create awesomeness in our lives. I look at how if we live too much in either the past or the future, we can create unhelpful patterns in our lives that do not serve the visions and aspirations of who we want to be. Then, through this awareness of the present moment, we can make choices that better serve us.

Being Powerfully Present

Mastering others is strength; Mastering yourself is true power. (Lao-tzu[7])

By giving yourself permission to be powerfully present, you can begin to break down the interpretations and beliefs that you have about your past and your future that hold you back. As a result, the power these thought patterns have on you will start to diminish.

Before I continue with discussing being in the present moment, I want to briefly explore what it means to be powerful from my own personal perspective.

First, I want to ask some questions. What is power? What does it mean to be powerful? Where does power reside? How is it created? How is it expressed?

When it comes to power, many people will think of money, politics, corporations, religious institutions, and many other such things. This, to me, raises the question, What is our relationship to power? Is power something external to be acquired? Many would argue yes. From my perspective, however, this is a form of separation, a way of thinking that is illusory, a trick of the mind that is a product of the dualisms that dominate our society.

I want to put forward the idea that power is a part of all of us. We are indivisible from it, and it is completely a part of who we are. It is my belief that just by the fact alone that we exist, we are powerful. In the wholeness of our being, we have power. We derive and access our power through living from the present moment. The ability to be powerful exists within every one of us.

The issue for many of us, though, is that we do not see that we can take ownership of our personal power. We have not been taught that we are powerful; it is not a part of most regular curriculums of education. Some cultural and spiritual traditions teach this to us, but for a lot of people, it is not even something we would think about. I know that I didn't. To me, the idea of being powerful was something for other people, for those I saw in the news or for people who were rich or popular. At times, the idea of being powerful also seemed like an unattainable fantasy that existed only in the realm of fiction, movies, and comic books.

I have learned, though, that we have also sometimes given away our power to circumstances, memories, or even other people. In some cases, we may have experienced our power being suppressed through external circumstance. For example, maybe acts of violence were committed against us or those we care about, or maybe we have had things imposed on us against our will. It may be hard to imagine accessing our innate power when circumstances such as these surround us. It can be done, though.

A personal example for me of finding my power in a difficult situation was after my car accident. I had left the hospital and was living in a shared house with two friends. I was still building up the muscles in my right leg for walking and had progressed from using crutches to using a cane. I was also spending most of my time in the house on my own. I used to go out to dance clubs regularly with my friends prior to the car accident, and I missed this socialization and the energy I used to get from dancing. I was feeling right sorry for myself. And then it dawned on me that my cane did not need to stop me. It was only my thoughts that were getting in the way of going out and enjoying myself. Now I may have anxiety when I go out, but if I push through it, it often goes away, and I can enjoy myself.

I think most people, though, live in a state of either recognising our power or not recognising our power. Just because we may not be feeling our power or seeing it in our lives does not mean it is not there. Awesome things start to happen for us when we embrace the power that we gain from living in the present moment. Even if is as simple as suddenly becoming aware of the scent of flowers or the familiar and comforting smell of someone you love. These everyday things can have an extraordinary effect on our lives as they can calm us, focus us, improve our emotional states, and positively impact our interactions with others.

Being too much into the future or too much into the past can accentuate the idea and belief of separateness. Feeling separate from things or people, for some of us, can generate fear and suffering. I know in my life that when I have felt separate and apart from the people I feel closest to I have caused myself to needlessly suffer. I also know now that when I am present, I am more easily able to feel connected to other people and things even if they are hundreds or thousands of kilometres away. It is quite an extraordinary process for me now that I think about it. When I am present, I feel whole. And when I feel whole, I feel intimately connected to those things that are important to me even if they are currently on the other side of the world. This process transforms my sadness or longing into joy or contentment.

Now, I will not deny there are people and institutions that have major influence over our experiences of what power is. However, the influence they exert does not have to create a powerful hold over our inner beings. When I contemplate this I think of Victor Frankl's book, *Man's Search for Meaning.*[8] If you do not know this book, I highly recommend it. The book is about his personal experience of surviving the concentration camps of Nazi Germany. He refers to the world of the mind and emotion. It is within this world of mind and emotion that people found their power to survive in horrific circumstances. To me, this exemplifies how people with an extreme physical power, including weapons that could kill, were not able to exert complete power and influence over everyone. The power of their guns did not completely destroy the spirits of all the people. Those who found inner power were able to find creative ways of surviving, of keeping their spiritual faith, and of maintaining their internal hope that they would make it through those intensely horrible circumstances. In Frankl's book, some people were able to continue as their personal paths were to approach their situations on a day-to-day basis. This is what gave them the meaning they needed to continue and survive.

Actually overcoming adverse situations often calls on people to be mindfully present and engage in life from a perspective of taking it day by day, hour by hour, or even minute by minute. If you have or someone you know has overcome addiction or come through a serious illness, you may know what I am referring to.

If We Are in the Wrong Tense, We Become Tense.

The Past

The past, though significant, in reality is actually only a memory we experience in the present moment. The past being experienced as a memory means we can choose how we want to learn from the past. We can also choose how we want to be emotionally invested in our experiences. In other words, from the present moment we have a choice as to whether a past experience is something that we can let get in the way of experiencing the beauty that is before us and getting in the way of reaching our goals and dreams. Or it can be something we can learn from that will assist us in our life journey and in obtaining our goals and dreams.

Exercise

What from the past do you still tend to focus on that gets in the way of what you desire to achieve right now?

The key message with the past is that we often get stuck thinking about past events over and over and over again and again and again. Our thinking about these past events can then create unhelpful repetitive patterns that may not serve us.

If we go back to the story of what happened to me around the car accident, I used to think about those incidents repeatedly. So much so that it was getting in the way of forming relationships. In fact, one woman I was dating found this very difficult, and my obsession with ruminating on the car accident was something that definitely got in the way of us having a better connection. In retrospect, this has now became a lesson for me. By being stuck in the past, I created the circumstance that made me miss things that were potentially positive and good for me in the present moment.

Another example of how being stuck in the past gets in the way for me is when I have had a disagreement with my wife. Well, let's be truthful here; when I have had full-blown arguments with her. Sometimes, I still have the tendency to remember and bring up real or imagined past slights against me. This then gets in the way of us working out what is actually happening in the present. I am definitely getting better at this, and I have learned that my life is so much more awesome when I let go of these things. Through conversing with my wife instead of arguing, I have also discovered these slights were not intentional, and it was my imagination blowing things up bigger than they actually were. I was letting a false sense of pride get in the way of hearing what was being said to me. We still have our arguments, but the less I engage in unnecessarily bringing up the past, the easier it is for us to work through the present moment concerns.

As I have demonstrated from my life, it is often the negative, not-so-nice events that we get stuck on. We go over these events or even create the circumstance to relive them even when they did not serve us the first time. When I think about it, I find it quite absurd that I will sometimes bring up painful past experiences or create situations in which I can repeat them when originally these did not usually serve me. What works better for me is to explore these experiences and learn from them so that I do not have to always repeat them. Instead of arguing again with my wife, I can apologise for my poor behaviour and seek her assistance in understanding where she was coming from. The funny thing is when either of us engages in this approach, we always end up apologising to each other and entering a more loving and appreciative space. Isn't that awesome?

Some examples of the typical negative thought experiences that can be related to the past are,

- I was dumped.
- My manager did not like my work.
- I had a fight with my partner.
- I failed that test.
- I got into that car accident.
- I missed another episode of my favourite TV show.

Sometimes, however, we also get stuck on a desire to repeat good experiences from our past. We try to relive these things even though our circumstances and experiences have changed. This is another absurdity I have engaged in—trying to relive experiences that have been positive for me. As I enjoy live music, I have seen some amazing concerts. However, sometimes I have found myself going to see a band the second time, expecting the experience to be like the first time. I have realised now that this is ludicrous for me to do as it is not even going to be the same playlist, not the same night, not the same crowd, and so on. So how could the next concert possibly be like the first? In these cases, I have sometimes missed the opportunity to appreciate a brand-new experience of what was a great concert in its own right. This is not to say some bands didn't suck the second time I have seen them, but I can confidently say that sometimes I have missed the opportunities for awesome experiences in the present through trying to relive old, good experiences from my past.

A few examples of some positive experiences that could be repetitive are,

- There has never been a party quite like that one.
- I met the partner of my dreams that night, and I will never meet another like him or her again.
- This year's celebration has to be as good or even better than last year's.
- I aced that game.
- I scored wickedly on that test.

Something to bear in mind is that we can get into a habit of repeating the past in the present moment. We can get into this trap of the mind for both negative and positive experiences. Learn from our experiences instead of overthinking them or trying to repeat them can assist us with seeing what is awesome in the present moment.

The Future

The future is also something that exists in the mind. When I realise that the future is only something that exists in my imagination, I see how it is possible for me to choose what thoughts I would like to have for the future. I can also choose what emotions I want to have when I think about the future.

Exercise

What do you imagine about your future? You can think in terms of short, medium, or long term. Or if you are game, you can give some consideration to all three.

Sometimes we can also get stuck with thinking about the future. If we think about the future without grounding ourselves in the present, we can create things that can also inhibit us from reaching our goals. We can also become so preoccupied with the future that we miss important and awesome experiences occurring for us in the present moment. A good example of this for me is doing an excessive amount of planning for things. For instance, I have spent a lot of time thinking about what I want to achieve with my business, what I want to offer to people, and where I want my life to go. Of course this is fine, but what I wasn't doing was living in the present and taking the necessary actions that would lead me to these goals. Rather, at times I would just do more planning or (as is my habit) more refining of what I developed. If I was not careful, I could have spent ages and ages editing this book, for instance, instead of getting it done and out there to share with you. In fact, this just about happened, and I could still be in the same place, endlessly creating plans for the book of my dreams.

Another way that being focused on the future can inhibit us is that we try to reinvent the past with our thoughts about the future. We create fantasies about the future and about how it won't work, or we get obsessed with trying to think about a way to recreate those wonderful experiences from our past. There have been times when I have stopped myself from planning something because what I imagine for the future resembles a negative experience from the past. You see this often in workplaces where an idea was tried and did not work. Then later, when circumstances change, a variation of the same approach might be applicable but is not given consideration as the first time was a "failure" or whatever we want to label it. Of course, some ideas remain dead in the water, and we learn from them. But other times they are worth revisiting. Just because I burnt the dinner for a romantic evening with my wife does not mean that it will play out exactly the same way the next time I try.

Let's be clear. I am not saying don't dream or have goals for the future. Rather, let's work on bringing these goals into the present moment. Of course, we can be outrageous with our dreaming. In fact, I strongly encourage it. Dream wildly, dream big, and dream playfully. Just don't be forever in the fun of the fantasy, and remember to take steps towards making your dreaming a reality.

Another key item for me in regards to future planning is about not getting too attached to the outcome that I want to have. When I find my satisfaction in the present moment, in my movement towards my aspirations and dreams, I find that life flows much better for me. When I live from a present state of mind in regards to the future, my life feels more full and exciting. I may never reach all my dreams, but by having them and working towards them, I create great experiences for myself and lots of opportunities for new learning, new relationships, and new ways of expressing love in the world.

The Present

Exercise

What does it mean to you to be aware of the present moment?

To me, the present moment is the place of our personal power. We only ever truly exist in the present moment as the past exists in our memories and the future in our imaginations. Through cultivating an awareness of what is occurring in our lives in the present moment, we gain the personal power to create the kind of lives that we want to live. We are the most powerfully awesome when we are living from the present moment.

In reality, we are only ever in the present as the past and future are fantasies in our heads. Past experiences happened, but they are not happening right now. They are only in our memories and, in fact, a past experience shared with others can often be remembered in different ways. An example of this is my wife and I have two different stories about how we fell in love. It is quite funny to other people when we both get an opportunity to share our individual stories with them at the same time.

The only true reality we have is the one we are in at this present moment. There really can be nothing else but this present moment, and our minds trick us into thinking otherwise. We can easily get caught up in the types of patterns I have already discussed in this chapter. However, we can create new thought patterns around how we interpret and learn from our past experiences and how we create plans around our dreams for the future.

Now, the trick in regards to the future is that we are most powerful in our choices through living from the present moment. When we start to think of the future as something that is in the present moment, we create more opportunities to make our choices possible. This is a bit of a heady concept. But it goes something like this. If we are forever saying we want to have or be something, we create a constant mindset of wanting those things. When we have that mindset, we see life through the lens of always wanting and will often make choices that reinforce the idea and experience of wanting. However, when we start to say things from the space of "I am," we start to change our perspectives. Saying, "I am," is a way of grounding ourselves in the present moment.

For me, a good example is shifting from saying I want to be healthy to using the words, "I am healthy." The more I have said this to myself, the easier it has become to believe it. One result of this has been that this thinking has also made it easier for me to make healthy choices and engage in healthy activities more often, such as taking regular walks. For more on the power of the words "I am," you can read Dr. Wayne Dyer's writings.[9] To further explore the question of "Who am I?" you can read about Bhagavan Sri Ramana Maharshi.[10]

When we live from the present moment, we are also more aware of what is going on around us. I know that the more I practice living presently, the more awesome I feel about myself and the more extraordinary my life gets. I make better choices and am definitely less likely to react negatively to things. When I am present to what is around me, I see more beauty and more love in the world. I also see things within myself that I can learn from as well when I do this. There is another cool side effect I experience when being fully present; I am also filled with more energy to do things I desire to do.

Awareness Wakes Us Up

When we are truly aware, we are in the present moment. When we are present, we can enter into a state of heightened awareness, and this can have benefits for us. Through cultivating our awareness, we can become more grounded. We connect to the things around us, and this can be calming. From this calm place we can also engage in reflection and contemplate more clearly the choices that we have in our lives.

Another thing I have found is that as I have cultivated my awareness, I have started to recognise my helpful and unhelpful repetitive behaviours. I have come to see through this that it is often my repetitive thinking or behaviour that cause me angst. For instance, repeatedly going over the thought that I almost died caused me much pain until I realised that I could learn from the experience. I have learned that I can make a choice to be aware of the awesomeness and beauty that is in front of and within me. I have learned that the car accident I was in was a truly awesome and extraordinary thing. Instead of living in a state of feeling sorry for myself or using it as a badge of honour to impress others, I now draw lessons from it that help me to live my life in the now.

When thinking about awareness, I would like you to consider contemplating a piece of art. I have sometimes had the experience of looking at a piece of art for some time, or I had seen the same piece multiple times, and then suddenly, something new about it arises in my vision or contemplation of it. If you use your hands to explore tactile pieces of art, the same thing can happen where you discover a groove, an indentation, or a protrusion that you never noticed before as it was subtle. Suddenly, you have a new understanding of the piece. Our awareness can be just like this. One time you are contemplating something and then you suddenly notice something new or different, and a wonderful, new comprehension dawns upon you about yourself, another person in your life, or even the world in general.

Exercise

What are you aware of in your life that makes you feel good?

In something familiar, have you ever noticed something you did not notice before? How did this make you feel?

I mentioned previously that through cultivating our awareness, we start to recognise our repetitive behaviours. I write more on this in the next chapter. Right now, however, I would like to mention that our repetitive behaviours can serve us as well as hinder us.

There are those behaviours that have gone past their use-by date. At one point they helped us, and we creatively invented them to assist us. But now they are not so helpful. For example, when I was a child, I developed a habit, like a lot of children do, of annoyingly asking lots and lots of questions until I understood things. I must have been crazy-making to the adults around me. I know now that asking questions is still helpful for understanding, but I have also learned that sometimes it is better for me to just listen and accept. I am thinking right now of the expression, "flogging a dead horse." This is something my questioning can lead me to do, and I have come to learn that this does not always serve my best interests. Just ask my wife when I have asked her heaps of questions after a long day.

But we do also have those repetitive behaviours that are still helpful and can serve us well. A few good examples of this are doing regular exercises or eating healthfully.

Once we start to become aware of what we may repeatedly do, we can take steps to start cleaning our internal houses and move into a more awesome mindset that can lower stress and increase our happiness. Our awareness can help us to realise that we actually have choices in our lives, and with these choices, we can manifest our own outcomes, our own happiness and love, and our own awesomeness.

Practice Makes the Perfect Present

What I would like to do now is share with you some techniques that can assist in helping you to be in the present moment and to build your awareness.

The first technique I recommend is meditation. There are many forms of meditation, and a good deal of these forms can assist in building awareness and becoming present. Meditation is awesome in my estimation. I personally use it to get grounded, to relax, and to get focused on my day or things that I deem to be important.

One thing that is important to note is the more you practice meditating, the more benefits you can start to have from doing it. For me, my meditation practice is like a wave;

sometimes I engage in it daily, and sometimes I can go for days or weeks without even thinking about it. What is great for me, though, is that I have learned that if I am feeling unsettled, I can take even a few minutes to use meditation techniques to ground myself and become calmer. Sometimes this happens after certain experiences have occurred and sometimes as they are about to occur. The more I practice meditating, the more I am able to notice and become aware of cues that can unsettle me.

There are many forms of meditation to choose from. Find one that works for you, or maybe you already have one. If you have not meditated before, I can recommend two to try. The first one is based on Vipassana, or mindfulness meditation, techniques I have learned from teachers such as Satya Narayan Goenka[11] and Christopher Titmuss.[12] I will briefly outline a good starting point for the technique for you, but you can also easily get information and support on how to refine and develop your techniques from various teachers and schools. This is just a brief outline of a technique, and there are great teachers out there that can guide and support you.

Find a quiet place to meditate where you will not be disturbed. Have a seat on the floor or a cushion with your legs crossed. If that is too uncomfortable, you can use a chair or even lie down. Close your eyes, and take a few slow and deep breaths. As you do this, start to clear your mind. Thoughts will still come up, but that is okay as it is perfectly natural and happens for all of us.

After you have taken a few breaths, start to pay attention to your upper lip or nostrils. As you bring your attention to these places, become aware of your breath moving across your nose or lip. To start with, you can continue to take a few intentional breaths in order to get a feel for the sensation. Afterward, just let your breath go back to its natural rhythm. You can keep doing this for fifteen to thirty minutes to start with or an hour if you can make the time.

Now, thoughts and emotions will come to your attention as you do this. Let them come; do not resist them. Let them come and then let them pass and go. If your attention leaves your breath, just bring it back to your breath. That is okay as you practice focusing on your attention and awareness. Do not give yourself a hard time when your attention wanders, as it will. It does for me. If you open your eyes, this is fine, too. Again, do not give yourself a hard time. Just close them again and continue to pay attention to your breath. During the meditation, it is okay to reposition your body. As you practice, you will discover the need to reposition yourself less.

You can use a timer, clock, phone, or whatever to time your meditation and let you know when your time is complete. When it is time to finish, slowly bring your attention back to the room you are in, to your body, and so on. Then slowly open your eyes. Move slowly as you get up; do not rush into moving or doing your next activities. You may find you have a sensation in your legs during or after, and this is fine as well. If there is a sensation present, move your legs slowly, rub them gently if necessary, and do not rush into your movements.

The second meditation is more of one that helps to relax the body, and as a result, this can lead to a relaxing of the mind as well. Start in a similar way to the first mediation. Find a quiet place where you will be undisturbed. You can sit on a cushion, the floor, a chair, or even lie down if you choose. Close your eyes and clear your mind. It also helps to take a few deep, slow breaths when you do this. Now, first feel where you are sitting or lying down and where your body makes contact with the chair, cushion, or floor. Allow yourself to settle into that spot, and feel your body as you do this.

Move your attention to your toes, then to the bottom of your feet, and then to the top of your feet. Continue to do this process of moving your attention up your whole body, moving from your calves to your thighs, your buttocks, your back and chest, your arms and hands, and finally, your shoulders, neck, face, and head. Do this slowly as you do not need to rush. You can then move back down your body or go back to your feet and start over again. Do this multiple times. Again, you can do this for fifteen to thirty minutes.

A variation of this is to tighten your muscles as you move to them for just a few seconds and then release them. This variation is a good way to relax your muscles and can help with relaxing the mind as well. Like the first meditation, when you are done, slowly open your eyes, and take your time getting up.

Choose the Change,
Create the Practice,
Claim the Awesome.

The Change

As we become more grounded in the present moment and learn to live from that place of awareness, we can start to choose the change we want to see in our lives. This next section has a number of exercises for you to do. We will start the section with choosing a change that you would like to have in your life.

Exercise

At this point, I would like you to take a moment to choose a change you want to have in your life that would make your life more awesome. If you want to go a bit deeper, take your time with it. My change right now, as I am writing this book, is about being physically fit and healthy. You also do not have to choose a big change for yourself. Sometimes it is more effective to start with something small.

Write out your change.

Now take a look at what you have written. Close your eyes, and visualise this for just a few moments before we continue. Imagine this change as though it has already happened for you. Get in touch with how you feel about this change; how good it makes you feel. It is awesome that you have done this and thought about new ways of creating your awesomeness.

Okay, this takes us to our next point.

The Practice

This section is about creating the practice to assist with the change you want to create in your life. As the expression goes, practice makes perfect. Basically, what we are doing here is creating a set of actions that assists you with bringing this desired change into your awareness and the present moment. By having a regular, repeated practice, we create a new behaviour, and hence, we are on our way to creating new realities for ourselves.

Exercise

I would like you to take a moment to imagine a practice for the change you have imagined and visualised for yourself. In regards to my fitness goal, I have created a realistic goal of walking at least twenty minutes a day. A good key for practice is to choose something that is realistic. Ninety minutes a day in the gym is not something that fits into the goals for my life, but twenty to thirty minutes I can handle and fits nicely.

Take a few moments now to develop a practice for your change. Be realistic, but it is also okay to set the goal as a bit of a challenge. Think about things that can support you in your change as this can help. I have done a few things to support my change. I asked for my wife's support, bought comfortable shoes for walking and running, and I bought a pedometer to measure my steps. I aim for ten thousand steps a day. My steps are recorded through an app on my phone to help motivate me.

Write out your practice.

Your Awesomeness

The third point here is about claiming your awesomeness. What I mean by this is taking control of your change. You have moved from thought to words, and now I am talking about deeds or actions. To be truly awesome, we need to believe we are awesome and take action on it. So set a start time to take action on your practice. As this is an exercise, you may need to refine it, of course, but step into it, own it, and bring it into the present moment.

What I did was stage my start with my fitness goals. I set one week to buy the shoes and then I started to walk a bit each day. The week after was for buying the pedometer. I used this for a few weeks to get used to the activity. Then I started tracking my progress through an app to help with my motivation.

What Is Your Action?

Another thing you can do here is focus on an awesome thing that already exists in your life. You can then use this as your anchor point. Take some time to think about what this awesome thing is. It can be an activity, an event, a feeling, and so on. For me, I think of how awesome it is that I have a supportive wife and supportive friends and family in my life. This anchor point is great for when I start to feel discouraged or think that what I want to achieve may be too hard. In fact, I have a few anchor points that help me in my journey.

What Is Your Awesome Anchor Point?

If you are finding it difficult to create your change or engage in your actions, if you are feeling discouraged and so forth, go to this anchor point. Your awesome anchor is there to remind you that you are already awesome and that the new awesome thing you want to achieve is possible.

Chapter 4

Repetitive Behaviours

Through reframing my repetitive behaviours, I can nurture my wisdom and fuel my creativity.

We now look at how, through cultivating the awareness I discussed in the last chapter, we can start to recognise the repetitive behaviours that no longer serve us. When we start to recognise unhelpful behaviours, we begin to observe how they no longer serve us. When this begins to occur, we can start to think about them in new and different ways. This can assist us in creating awesomeness in our lives.

On the other side of the coin, though, behaviours that we have labelled as bad habits can start to be seen as wise and creative choices that were made given the circumstances we were experiencing in our lives at the time. Our behaviours can then become signposts that we can choose to learn from. They can provide us with personal lessons and help us to understand how we can be the person we want to be. So when we look at how we have crafted our repetitive behaviours, we can start to realise that we were actually being quite extraordinary at the time they were created.

It can be quite an extraordinary thing to shift our personal interpretations of our behaviours as we often experience these interpretations as being the absolute truth. But as I have learned through self-reflection and discussion with others, truth is not always as it seems, and there are often many ways to interpret an experience. Of course, there is what I think of as the root experience of a situation, I am typing this book on my computer right now, but what can change is the meaning I choose to associate with this action.

Something even as simple as watching a movie or reading a book can elicit multiple responses. Who hasn't enjoyed watching a movie or reading a book and discovered that someone else in their lives thinks it is rubbish when you have held it in high regard? The truth would be that you both read the book or watched the movie, but the way you experienced them is open to interpretation. At times, our lives can be like this.

I was in a horrific car accident, and someone died. Since then, I have had many interpretations of what this has meant to me. Right now the one that makes the most sense and serves me more fully is that it was a key trigger point in my life that has led me to realise I can choose to lead an extraordinary life and see that I am living in a world of awe.

Exercises

What habits do you have? They can be what you think of as good or bad habits; it does not matter.

Which behaviours do you engage in that you feel hold you back?

Stuck Like a Skipping CD

When I was first going to title this section I thought I might use, "Stuck Like a Broken Record," but then I realised that was a bit dated. I am a teen of the eighties, and records or cassettes were the way to play music until near the end of the decade, when compact discs—CDs—started to become more popular and affordable. Even that is dated now as we can download or stream music in the blink of an eye. Now that I have personally dated myself, I will promptly continue. Either saying, however, is a good metaphorical description of how we can get caught up in repeating our behaviours.

So what happens when we start to feel stuck or stopped? One of the things that can occur when we feel stuck is get caught up in repetitive behaviours that we originally created to make us feel better, to distract us from something that was maybe too hard for us to deal with at the time, or to fill an unfulfilled need.

Why do we continue to engage in some of our repetitive behaviours when we may say to ourselves that we want to be different in relation to behaviours or habits we do not like anymore? One thing that happens is that our brains get trained to reuse the coping behaviours we created to respond to difficult situations. Then, when we are in new situations that we interpret as being similar to that first experience, we use that behaviour again to get us through the situation. If it worked for us once, why not again? So, as we encounter circumstances that may seem identical to the first experiences, we react in the same way. Sometimes this is a correct and a good way to be. For instance, we may learn to recognise danger that could physically harm us or even kill us, so we create a behaviour to avoid or navigate that circumstance. Then, as we encounter other dangerous situations, we have a good way to respond that can hopefully keep us safe.

Sometimes we engage in repetitive behaviours that we are happy about. Some become a part of our normal routines and give our lives security and/or meaning. Then there are some we do not like.

Creative Adjustment: A Way of Reframing Our Self-Portrait

When I was studying Gestalt therapy, I learned a term that resonated with my soul and is still with me regularly: "creative adjustment." I have already alluded to this by talking about our repetitive behaviours as being creative choices. This way of looking at past experiences has been and still is powerful for me. It has assisted me in reducing my anger, learning to forgive, and lessening my shame.

My interpretation of this theory is that throughout our lives—and particularly when we were younger—we encountered situations that were difficult or unexpected. When these situations arose, we were unsure how to react, so we had to create a response to adjust to the circumstances and learn to deal with them. What we did was use the creative parts of our minds to adjust to the situation and engage in a behaviour that would ultimately try to protect us or make us feel better or safer. Without realizing it, we cleverly made awesome creative adjustments to our lives to assist ourselves. Isn't that an awesome and amazing way to think of how we created some of our behaviours?

Now, within Gestalt therapy, the definition of "creative adjustment" is much fuller and more in depth. I am sharing with you a personal interpretation that I feel is relevant for what I am discussing in this chapter. For a definition from some of the creators of Gestalt therapy, you can read from Perls, Hefferline, and Goodman.[13] For more recent short interpretations, you can read Edwin C. Nevis[14] or Yontef and Fuhr.[15]

As I mentioned earlier, sometimes situations arise that are similar or remind us of those initial experiences we creatively adjusted for. Then, at some point, we choose to react in that way again because it worked for us the first time. Pretty smart, I reckon.

But as we get older, we sometimes start to look at those behaviours and see them as not so positive. We may even label them as bad habits that we no longer want. We forget or do not even realise that this behaviour was, in fact, a very clever reaction to a situation where we may have been out of our depths. So instead of seeing the behaviour as something that just no longer serves us, we see it as being a part of us, as being a bad habit that we use to give ourselves a hard time. These habits may also be things that will sometimes trigger our embarrassment or shame.

If we observe that the behaviours we currently do not like were originally good things for us, we can start or even choose to see them as no longer shameful parts of us but, rather, as patterns that just do not serve us anymore. When we do that, we can start to choose to react differently. This is a way that we can move into claiming our personal power. We can see that we were awesome through our adaptability and creative thinking and then reclaim our awesomeness by reframing our experiences and making new choices that serve who we want to be.

For example, maybe as a child your mother and father argued with each other loudly, and you found this distressing. So you ran away to your room and disappeared into books or games, or you started to be noisy yourself to distract yourself or them from what was happening. Both of these types of responses would have been very creative ways of dealing with what you can imagine would be a difficult situation for a child. Then, if the parents had their own patterns of arguing, the child might repeat this behaviour again and again until it became a habitual coping behaviour.

Then, as the child gets older, the use of this behaviour may become a coping mechanism in his or her own relationships by either running away, escaping, or being noisy. It might not serve them anymore and could potentially get in the way of what might be a productive or positive relationship. The individual might also start to feel embarrassment or even shame over engaging in this behaviour. However, if the person starts to recognise that this was an old pattern that was the result of learning to cope with a difficult circumstance, he or she may choose to respond differently. Of course, this may take practice; I know I have needed to practice this. These were some of my types of reactions that I created to deal with, not my parents arguing, but with stressful situations I encountered as a child where I felt helpless.

I still work on identifying my own patterns and behaviours. Sometimes I need support and feedback from others to help me identify these. For example, I have a habit of swearing when I put myself under stress. Sometimes I also raise my voice. I can see that this is a very old habit for me. I remember doing this from a young age; maybe the swearing started from as early as when I was eleven or twelve years old or so. I can see that this was a strategy I adopted at a young age to get myself heard and noticed when I felt I was being ignored.

When I look back on it, this was a very effective way as a child to get attention. Of course, my parents did not put up with this, but I would have to say that this behaviour persisted and is still with me in some way today. It can still create awkward situations for me, but I have learned that I do not need to be that way. I am also discovering that as I react in that way less and less, the more I become aware of what I am doing in the present moment. I recognise in myself that being loud no longer serves who I want to be. I have realised that what I did as a child was find a creative way to get an unmet need for attention met.

Through recognising this behaviour, I was able to think back to when it more or less started. You do not always need to find the first incident. What is important to recognise is what you creatively did to cope with difficult circumstances. Then, through recognising this pattern, we are able to see how we creatively adjusted ourselves to react to things in a way that assisted us with having an unmet need met.

For some people there may be a highly distressing or traumatic circumstance that created the need to creatively cope. If this is the case for you, as I mentioned earlier in the book, you may want to consider visiting an accredited professional who can assist you with working through the thoughts and emotions that surround the memories of such experiences. I have done this, and I feel there is no shame in seeking support from someone who has been properly trained to work with you on something of this nature. I know from personal experience that I have benefited immensely from visiting with psychologists and therapists.

So when we start to recognise our repetitive behaviours and how they started, we can start to reframe what they mean to us. Behaviours we label as bad habits can start to be seen as wise and creative choices that were made given the circumstances that we were in. As we can see that the past is in our memories, we can start to look at these behaviours in a new, more productive way.

Recognising and reframing our repetitive behaviours are key to understanding our own wisdom and can assist us with unlocking our creativity. My most straightforward way of describing reframing is that it is a process where we look at an experience or behaviour and choose to see it in a different way, one that will serve us better. When we start to recognise our repetitive behaviours and how they started, we can start to reframe what they mean to us and how we allow them to affect us. Through reframing, we start telling a different story about our life in the present moment.

After we start to recognise that the choices we made were creative, we can then start to choose what behaviours serve us and which no longer serve us. Our behaviours can then also be seen as signposts in our lives. One signpost that I have is recognising that when I start to feel hot and clammy, I am at a point where I could easily get frustrated and even angry or defensive. This is an old pattern I have from childhood; the temper tantrum, so to speak. When I am able to see these signs within myself, I can choose to react differently. This has taken me practice, and, in fact, I still need to practice this one. However, I can honestly say that I am getting better at it, or at the very least, quickly realising what I have done so that I can go and make amends after engaging in an unhelpful behaviour.

I want to challenge everyone to start looking at what they see as bad behaviours as clever adjustments made to cope when nothing else was working. I would love for everyone to give themselves a good pat on the back and say that "These behaviours were good things that happened at the time they were created as I was coping in the best and most creative way that I could."

Exercises

1. The first part of the exercise is to go back to some of the behaviours you identified at the beginning of the chapter, and choose one. Of course, you can choose a new behaviour if you like.
2. Look at this behaviour through the lens of creative adjustment. How was this behaviour creative for you, and what type of situations was it assisting you with?
3. When you look at this behaviour in the context of your present situation, does it still serve you? It might. It could be a wonderful behaviour that serves you well, but it might also no longer serve you.
4. If this behaviour no longer serves you, what can you do differently when similar circumstances arise for you?
5. Go back to the exercises at the end of the last chapter if you want to take further action to create change around behaviour. As a reminder, the final exercises at the end of the last chapter consisted of the following three things.

    Choose the change.
    Create the practice.
    Set the action.

Pain, Panic, and Pride

When I start to look at behaviours that I see as no longer serving me or other people I engage with, I start to observe how they seem to fall into three general categories for my life: pain, panic, and pride. This by no means is a comprehensive generalisation of the circumstances surrounding how and why we engage in some of our repetitive behaviours. But it is one that serves a function for me in learning about my behaviours. It is a framework that helps me to understand my behaviours and assists me in shifting them. It appears to me that these three categories are often the catalysts that helped to form the repetitive behaviours I have in the first place.

Avoiding Pain

When we were younger, we may have found ourselves in situations where we faced a threat of emotional or physical pain. When this happened, we needed to find ways to cope with those experiences. We needed to creatively find ways to avoid or forget the pain we were facing. As we did, we created awesome behaviours to cope. However, as we get older we sometimes use these same behaviours to avoid potential pain when new responses would serve us better.

Calming the Panic

Other times we may have found ourselves in situations where we started to panic. These circumstances created situations where we found ourselves in states of anxiety. We seemed to feel like we were losing control or had no control at all. We then created responses that helped to calm this sense of panic, those feelings of being out of control.

Pride: Shifting the Shame

Another common response to situations is to sometimes feel shame over actions that we have engaged in. When we felt this shame, we created ways to avoid or ignore it. Sometimes this would be about wounded pride when we were much younger. Our shame then led us to create new repetitive behaviours so that we would no longer feel the pain.

I would like to say here that shame and guilt are things that can greatly influence our behaviours. As I gain more experiences in my life, I see more and more how to differentiate shame from guilt. It is an ongoing process of understanding for me, and in the past few years, my thinking on shame has shifted.

Currently, to me, guilt is a function of reflecting on a personal action and coming to understand that what I did was not appropriate for the situation. I might feel bad about it but at the same time realise that I can make amends for it or look to avoid doing it again in the future. Guilt is a function that can serve us. An example for me was the first time I travelled through India. At some places where I ordered food it was customary to eat using your fingers. I found myself using both my hands at times. Then, not long after arriving, a fellow traveller informed that it was tradition to use the right hand predominantly. I felt some guilt over this. However, it was a productive guilt as it assisted me with fitting into a cultural norm that had a potential for creating awkward situations for me or others.

The use of guilt can also be one way for us to learn about ourselves. When we start to notice that we are feeling guilty about something we have done, this can act as a signpost for us to look at what we have been doing and evaluate the situation for ourselves. I am not referring, however, to those times when people use guilt to manipulate others into doing what they want them to do. This form of using guilt can be unhelpful and is, in my estimation, actually someone trying to use the function of shame to get his or her way.

Of course, we can hold onto something we feel guilty about for a long time, and it can start to become shame. From my perspective, shame is more about holding a personal belief about myself. Not just a belief about an action I have done but, rather, a belief about the person I am behind the action.

Some amazing insight into these distinctions between guilt and shame can be found in the writings of Brené Brown. In particular, I recommend an article she has posted on her website titled, "Shame vs. Guilt,"[16] which is an excerpt from her book *Daring Greatly*.

The reason I am discussing pain, panic, and pride/shame is that these things can be used to help us identify why we created the repetitive behaviours that may no longer serve us. If we apply these ideas to our behaviours, we may start to understand them better and then when this occurs, we can start to more easily make the choices that better serve us in the present.

Opportunity Knocks on Signposts

My behaviours are signposts in my life that I have chosen to learn from. They provide me with lessons and help me to understand how I can be the person I want to be.

As I start to track my behaviours and reframe them, I have chosen to start seeing these as signposts for my life as well. I can see where some of my behaviours have originated and where I have started to shift them. From this, I have learned lessons about what worked for me in the past and what does not work for me now. From these lessons, I can learn to identify when circumstances arise that might trigger that behaviour. These signposts can become a part of our awareness. As we travel through our lives, we can recognise the experiences that continue to trigger us and then choose more productive and helpful reactions that better serve us.

Exercise

What are some of the signposts in your life?

What can you learn from these signposts?

Chapter 5

Honouring Emotions

*When I honour and respect all of my emotions,
I can learn to shift those that hold me in
unhelpful and repetitive patterns.*

Through learning to honour all of our emotions, we are
also learning how to experience the full range of who we
are. As we practice this, we acquire skills that can assist us
with shifting away from unhelpful repetitive patterns and
shame processes that can inhibit us. As we become aware of
these processes, we can start to understand our behaviours
in a new and different way. Then our shame starts to lose
its meaning, and this opens up a new way of thinking about
our emotions that can lead to more awesome experiences for
us. These new personal processes can assist us with seeing
how we can make different choices in our lives that are more
in alignment with who we want to be.

I have learned that honouring all of my emotions allows
me to experience the full range of who I am and who I can
be. Through respecting the diverse emotions that I feel, I

can begin to shift away from the shame processes that can inhibit me. All my emotions are a part of who I am, and by honouring this, I can truly say that I have learned to experience a fuller range of myself and the extraordinary possibilities that are available to me in my life. When we honour and respect all our emotions, we are giving ourselves wonderful and beautiful opportunities to experience the full expression of who we are.

When I contemplate my emotional range, I can see how it has been important to allow myself to feel all of my emotions, in particular, those that have made me feel uncomfortable. A good personal example is that after the car accident I described earlier, I used to keep my anger and shame about what happened at bay. I used to hold them apart from me. I did not let myself feel them, and unfortunately, this sometimes meant that my anger arose at inappropriate times and was directed towards those people I care about. Then one day while I was attending the experiential portion of the psychotherapy course I studied, I was given the opportunity to look at my anger and shame in a new way. This new way was simply giving myself permission to be angry. Until that point, the feelings of anger I had around the car accident used to make me feel very uncomfortable. I also used to feel that I was not allowed to be angry at the person who caused the accident as he died in it and paid that ultimate price. Logical or illogical, I felt a lot of shame about the death of this man. When I learned that I could allow myself to be angry about what happened and then let myself feel that anger, it was like a great weight was lifted from my shoulders. Once I accepted my anger and gave it a voice, I discovered that this particular anger that kept reappearing for me started to dissipate and allowed me space to start exploring my own trauma around the car accident. Subsequently it led me on a path towards learning what it actually means to engage in forgiveness.

Anger is an emotion that is often seen as something that we do not want to have at all. Some people have strong ethics about never showing any anger. What I have observed is that anger is actually a very important emotion. It gets us in touch with our principles and values; it can also let us know when someone has crossed our boundaries. One example in my life is that I can feel anger over reading about or seeing in the news incidents where people have been tortured. When I look more closely into this, I see that I have a strong belief in human rights. This is a value for myself that I learned through exploring my anger.

There is an appropriate time for us to feel grief, to feel anger, to feel happiness, and so on. As our emotions come up, we can see them, feel them, and then let them pass through us to make space for new emotions to arise.

I believe that happiness and positivity definitely have a place in terms of creating change and discovering awesomeness in our lives. I do not think, though, that forcing ourselves to be happy or using it to cover up other emotions is helpful. We have to be careful not to use happiness and positivity as a bandage to cover up those raw emotions that are so important. I discuss more of this later in the chapter.

At the same time, I want to say that our other emotions are also awesome. An example of an emotion that some people say they do not want to experience very much of is grief. In fact, I have worked with people who have kept their grief so far at bay that it has come to define who they currently are. They find it difficult to lead their normal, everyday lives as a result. I feel for these people as I have experienced grief in my life. and it was hard for me at times. I can only imagine what it is like for people who are still in grief years after losing a loved one, for instance. Grief is not a linear process and is unique to each person.

Grief to me, though, can truly be an awesome thing. At the core of it, grief really is an expression of love that can enhance our experiences of who we are. Grief is a natural and appropriate emotion. If someone close to us dies, I believe it is good to grieve as to me, it is an expression of my love and affection for this person. Like so many things, grief has its own time frame. For some people, it is a shorter process; for others, it can take a very long time. In either case, the grief can stay with us our whole lives in some form, depending on what may trigger it in us. For example, I have contended with the deaths of all of my grandparents. However, occasionally at times such as Christmas, I still think of them and grieve their loss.

If grief turns into a repetitive behaviour that no longer serves who you are and what you want to be doing in your life, maybe having a closer look at it could be useful. Sometimes self-reflection helps. Some people may need support from others close to them or, in some cases, from a professional in order to find their way through the experience. Having worked with people in bereavement, I know grief can be quite a complex thing for some people. They may need some guidance through it from people with experience and expertise in the area. Some people also benefit immensely from peer-to-peer support from others who have also been through a personal grieving process.

Grief also helps me to learn more about who I am. When one of my grandfathers died, I learned that I had a new capacity for compassion and empathy. His death taught me that I can forgive other people. More important, it was one of my first lessons in realising that forgiveness is more about my own internal process rather than about people who are external to me. I explore forgiveness later in the book.

Exercise on Emotion

The following exercise is one I have adopted and adapted from Dave Logan. I briefly met Dave and heard him speak at an amazing event called Awesomeness Fest put on by a company called MindValley. Dave has researched and currently teaches about tribal leadership.[17]

Think of an incident that causes you to feel lots of anger. Maybe it is something that makes you feel indignant or offended. It could be something that has happened to you personally, or it could be something that you have seen in the news or online. It can even be something that has happened to someone you know. Write it down.

Now, I would like you to focus in on why this incident has made you feel angry. Explore the reasons within yourself, even if they seem illogical and irrational, and write them down.

Look again at the reason you got angry. Is there something there that makes sense to you? This could be a signpost pointing you towards one aspect of your value system.

If there is not something there that makes sense, you can repeat the process again and again. This will help you identify the value that was crossed and led you to getting angry. When you repeat the process, read what you wrote about what made you angry, and this time look for what is important in that statement to you. After you do that, you might start to get some insight. This can sometimes take a while, and you can play with focusing on different aspects of what you have written. You may discover that the experience links to more than one core value as well. When I did this exercise around a few experiences, it highlighted some values that I had not given voice to in a while. It reminded me that I have a strong value around human rights.

Sometimes we may also discover that we do not have a reason to be angry that makes sense to us now. Or we realise that it used to make sense to us at one point in our lives, but it is no longer relevant for us. Through exploring our anger in ways like these, we can start to identify more unhelpful, repetitive patterns in our lives.

You may want to do this exercise again to explore another emotion. You could go back and look at an experience, for instance, that made you happy. This could also potentially point you in the direction of some of your core values.

Of course, if we stay in any of these emotions for a very long time, they become repetitive behaviours as discussed in the last chapter. Then they can start to hold us in a pattern that may not be helpful to us anymore. However, as I have been saying, we need to remember these behaviours and emotions were all awesome things originally. When we look at them with awareness, we can now choose new, extraordinary ways of being in the world and with other people.

Vulnerability

As I am discussing emotions, I thought I would also talk more about how I engage with my vulnerability. There have been many times in my life when I have felt vulnerable— getting lost as a child, doing a public speaking engagement, trying new experiences, and so on. When I feel ashamed, it sometimes results from having a sense of vulnerability in a given situation. However, embracing my vulnerability has also been a way to create awesomeness in my life. When I have embraced it and allowed myself to experience the emotions that are associated with vulnerability, great things have happened for me.

Vulnerability is something that can also hold us back if we let it. Sometimes when I think of this, I think of the saying, "Once bitten twice shy." For instance, when I have been exposed to vulnerability in a way that was not a good experience for me, it has caused me to rethink engaging in certain behaviours, actions, and so on that were similar to that first experience. Feeling vulnerable can be a scary thing. No one generally likes to feel vulnerable.

One sign of me engaging in my vulnerability is in the lead-up to things like public speaking or key engagements with other people, especially when I am not feeling completely confident. This manifests for me as nervousness, and as I mentioned at the beginning of the book, I have now started to recognise that there is anxiety involved with this as well. This started for me at a very early age, when I was in grade six of public school. For an assignment we had to do a speech, and I was very nervous and scared. Then after giving the speech, I took the teacher's feedback as criticism. It did not help that the other kids laughed as the teacher was giving it. I was a highly sensitive child, and I now recognise that I am also a highly sensitive adult. However, now I see it as a strength and something that assists me. As a result of this experience as a child, it was years before I was willing to do public speaking again.

I often feel nervous as a result of anticipating being in what I may perceive as a vulnerable situation, such as public speaking. When I have resisted the nervousness or tried to push it down inside me, this has prevented me from having a great experience. However, when I have accepted my nervousness and allowed myself to experience my vulnerability, my creativity starts to flow, and I can actually transition into a state of enjoying the situation. I now recognise that the old, repetitive pattern of nervousness does not serve me anymore and that now I can do something about it. Avoiding public speaking was my way of keeping myself safe and containing the rawness of my sensitivity. It served me well for years, until I learned the skills to be able to comfortably be the centre of attention in ways that are appropriate for me. I still may free fall into public speaking in some ways, but now I have the skills and awareness to be able to it.

When I think of feeling nervous, I think of the teachers I had at the Sydney Gestalt Institute. They used to say that nervousness and excitement are similar energy. For example, the body can react in the same way to these seemingly separate emotional states with things like heightened breathing and clammy hands. Learning to reframe my emotions in this way has assisted me through many situations where I was feeling nervous prior to certain activities. To be honest, I still feel nervous about engaging in many activities. However, now when I am in awareness of this, I can honour the nervousness. Then when I remember to, I can reframe it in a way that lessens the overwhelming feelings that I can sometimes have. Changing my personal perspective and interpretation of a situation assists with decreasing any anxiety I may be having and can lead me into having a more fulfilling experience.

I would like to put forward—like people such as Brené Brown in her TED Talk, "The Power of Vulnerability"— that vulnerability can lead us to wonderful and unexpected things. I think honouring vulnerability is very important. I have seen time and time again how when I honour it and allow it to be exposed it can create awesome things in my life. I want to say here that vulnerability is both awesome and extraordinary.

Sometimes when I have been in conflict with other people, I come into awareness that I am feeling vulnerable. Then I will often find that I am faced with a choice. I can either push the vulnerability down or choose to expose it. I have been discovering more and more that when I expose it and am also being non-judgemental of the other person, I can sometimes affect a shift in the situation. Being non-judgemental is part of the key here because when I have done this and express judgement of the other person, he or she will then judge my vulnerability, creating a situation where we end up feeding off each other's judgements. Through expressing my vulnerability, people start to see more of who I am and what I am thinking and feeling. Then, extraordinarily, other people sometimes start to show their vulnerability to me. I have learned that when I do this, the tension will usually start to dissipate, and a mutually respectful understanding will begin to emerge.

Of course, there are times when expressing vulnerability may not be the wisest or even the safest thing to do. In a bullying situation, for instance, this could potentially spurn the bully on to more aggressive behaviour. What is important to do is to observe the situation, and figure out what the fear is that is causing the vulnerability to arise. Once you start identifying the situation and the circumstances surrounding it, you can then make a decision that is best for you.

If it is a situation that may cause you harm, your fear and vulnerability are probably justified and could be serving you in a good way. If that is the case, you can still embrace these emotions and thoughts within yourself. As you do this, the safest course of action may more easily occur to you. I find that when I accept the emotion and allow it to flow through me, I start to think more clearly. I may still be in an unsafe situation, but I am able to choose a more appropriate response for me. The vulnerability and nervousness in a situation like that can serve as another signpost, letting you know what courses of action may have a better outcome for you.

It may not be safe to expose your vulnerability in a dangerous situation, but the insight that you gain from practicing emotional awareness may help you to identify a similar situation in the future. From this you may be able to identify the signs of it earlier and take action to potentially avoid it. This is a new and intentional way of creating a helpful repetitive behaviour to meet your needs.

As a therapist, I have seen when people expose their vulnerabilities in sessions, they can often start to feel differently about their situations. It is not always a magic bullet, but I have seen time and again how this can make a difference for both others and myself. Also, as a client of therapy myself, when I have felt safe and exposed my vulnerabilities to my therapist, I start to experience some of the changes I sought. When I have done this, I often feel an immediate difference in what I am feeling. It has been an extraordinary thing for me to learn that when I embrace those emotions, such as vulnerability or anger, I can create positive change in my life.

Happiness

I would like to talk now about happiness, given that I have been discussing emotions in this chapter. I was raised in a society where happiness is often seen as an external thing to be desired and obtained. Happiness in this context is seen as being separate from us, almost like an object that we can either possess or not possess. I have learned that happiness, though, is not external to me. Rather, it is something that is already within me. Happiness is something I can choose to get in touch with because it is already mine, and I do not need to seek it from other people or things. My happiness is something that is not reliant on things that are external to me.

Of course, we can still feel happiness and derive pleasure from experiences with other people. When we do this in relation to things that are external to us, I feel they are providing us with a means to get in touch with ourselves and our emotions and experiences. Being in situations that cause me happiness is a process for me of having a fuller, loving experience of who I am and the world around me.

I want to be clear in saying that I do not think that we need to choose happiness at all times in our lives. I believe we need to make space for us to experience the full awesome range of all our feelings. Happiness is just one of many emotions that we have. What is important for me here, though, is that I can learn to choose to be happy when it will serve me better.

A good, straightforward example for me is looking at something like road rage. When I am driving my car, there have been times when I have gotten really angry with people who have cut me off, for instance. When I have gotten angry over a situation like this, it sometimes affects that part of the day for me. When I look at these types of circumstances, I realise that this does not need to be the case for me. In a situation like this, I can actually choose to be happy and understanding of the situation as this will serve me better in terms of not allowing the situation to ruin the moment or even part of my day.

There are also times choosing happiness may not be appropriate for me, though, such as when grieving the loss of a family member. If I forced it in this situation, my grief would still be within me even though I was being or acting happy. The grief would still need an outlet.

I have observed how in my life I have often externalised happiness and turned it into something to be pursued and obtained. Sometimes this pursuit of happiness still occurs for me, and I need to remind myself that the happiness can be here and now in the present moment within me. In fact, I would argue, that if I am creating an experience of always pursuing happiness that is exactly what I will find and create for myself—an ongoing pursuit of happiness that is seemingly elusive. As I am always in the state of pursuing as opposed to experiencing happiness, it will always be separate from me within that context. In essence, if I am looking for happiness, I create the reality of "looking" as opposed to creating a reality for myself where I am "experiencing."

Another realisation I have had about happiness is that it is not something to be imposed on others. We know people and institutions that tell us what we need to do in our lives in order for us to find and experience happiness. I have found that what happens for me is that happiness loses some of its vitality when it is something that I am told to do. I want to note that this is different from having a shared experience of reality or even being happy for someone as we observe them achieving something and share in that joy with them.

What I am referring to are those times when I have allowed myself to be compelled into a situation where I am supposed to be happy according to someone else's standards and then discover that the situation is not as enjoyable as I was told it would be. This does not mean, though, that people or institutions are "wrong." Rather, they show me paths that I can choose to follow. As I choose a path to explore, it either resonates with who I am or who I am not. To me, the process of following a path to happiness is one of internalisation, where I examine the path, give it a chance, and then see if it is a path that works for me. When the path becomes more personal, it has more meaning for me. For me, the key is that happiness is now something that comes from within me, something that I can express and feel within myself and then express externally if I so choose. From my perspective, this is an awesome way of being as I can choose the course of my happiness and how I want to share it with the world.

One revelation I have had is that happiness is not an answer; it is a state of existence for me that is natural, much like love.

The more I look at my happiness, the more I allow it to be expressed in my life without pursuing it. And the more I do not force it, I start to see and realise that it is there within me to be experienced when I choose to instead of making it reliant upon external factors.

When I look at my life in this way, I understand and experience that happiness is not separate from me but, rather, actually a part of me and, in fact, has always been a part of me. This is a concept that was hard for me to wrap my head around at first, and I often need to remind myself of this. But when I do, it sure makes my life much more awesome.

Empathy

In this next part I say a few words on empathy as this can sometimes influence people's emotional states. I have observed that when I am with other people, I can allow their moods to affect mine. Have you had this experience? I know I have. In cases of good experiences, this is generally not a problem for me. However, there have been times when I have allowed myself to adopt other people's anger, sadness, and frustration. When I have adopted other people's emotional states, it does not always help me or even assist the other person.

Of course we can have empathy and compassion in regards to what other people are feeling. In fact, it is very difficult not to sometimes. Where it can become a problem is when we adopt their behaviours in ways that are not appropriate to our own circumstances. If someone is angry with a co-worker, we can show understanding. But does it serve us to get angry with that person's co-worker and then potentially stay angry throughout the day as well? To show our support for our friend, we may express some anger over the situation, but at the same time, we need to use our awareness to determine if it will serve us to stay angry.

Sure, I can say that because my partner is upset or angry at something I am now angry; when he or she is happy, I am happy; when he or she is annoyed, I am annoyed, and so on. However, through my self-contemplation, I see this can sometimes be an absurd process for me. Just because someone I know has an emotion does not mean that I need to adopt it for myself. In fact, when I am able to be in awareness around this, I can see that often what is more useful in these situations is for me to sit in the emotion that is more relevant for me, and this can be of assistance to the other. To put it simply, how can I support my wife through something that is upsetting to her if I, too, am upset? Or to put another way, if my nephew has cut his hand and is hysterical, what good what it be for him if I was to adopt his hysteria? What would be more useful to him would be for me to remain calm and tend to his wound.

I want to note here that this does not mean that I do not feel we should not have empathy. To me, empathy is not about immediately adopting and hanging onto the other's feelings. To me it is about coming from a place of understanding and compassion for the other's situation. When we have emotional awareness, we can be awesome in the way that we support other people and ourselves.

Happiness as Action: Let's Make It a Verb

Okay, here we are. In this section, I want to challenge you to turn happiness into a verb, so my advance apologies to the grammatically correct masses of teachers, professors, students, readers, and so on. As we want to be expressions of awesomeness in our lives, we can take our conceptions of happiness out into the world. Let's not be dogmatic about happiness, but let's live it and lead by example. Our actions in part define us, so why not let them be expressions of love and happiness? When we share our happiness, we choose one of many powerful and awesome ways to build relationships, communities, and societies. As I choose to allow my happiness to flow into the world, I can see how it is one of the things that helps to strengthen the many relationships I have in my life. I explore relationships in further detail in the next chapter.

Exercise

Take a moment here to reflect again on happiness. Only this time, I would like you to think about what ways you express happiness in the world. Does this have an impact on others? How do others react? How do you feel when you express your happiness in the presence of others?

One thing that can come up when doing an exercise like this one is that people sometimes react negatively to expressions of happiness. They may say things like, "What are you so happy about?" or, "You have no right to be happy." Does any of this sound familiar?

My first response to this is to remember that we also have the capacity to hold multiple thoughts, reactions, and emotions within us at the same time. An example I will use here is when I have attended funerals for family members or friends. I feel sad that I have lost them—that my friends and family and I will no longer be able to have new experiences with them. To me, this is appropriate. But at the same time, I have feelings of happiness that can arise as I remember shared experiences with this person, or someone shares a funny story they have of the person. In these moments, the happiness comes out. I am feeling both happy and sad, both very real and important emotions.

Another thing I would say is that only we are responsible for our own emotions. Maslow says that we need to be, "independent of the approval and disapproval of others, and seek rather self-approval."[18] To me, this means that we can listen to what others have to say and respect their opinions as their own views, but in the end, we decide what is right for us. Of course we can choose to adopt others' opinions, and this is a perfectly natural way of learning and moving through life. But the key to me is that I am slowly, every day realising that my beliefs are my choices, and if I want to, I can change my mind or question and challenge them. It is ultimately up to me how I choose to express my beliefs.

I want to point out that I am not advocating complete individualism here. It is my belief that we are all interconnected, that our actions have consequences, and that we live in world of cause and effect. To me, part of making choices about things like happiness is to take ownership and responsibility for them, to weigh what these choices are, and to understand that I am a part of many communities of people that my actions will potentially have an impact on. Again, this might seem like a paradox, making decisions for myself but also considering community. I do not think that they are mutually exclusive. If I make good choices for myself, I can better serve my community. And at the same time, if I make considered choices to serve the community, this may also serve my life.

I want to suggest that as we embrace our happiness, we take it out into the world with us. How awesome would our lives be if we were more often open expressions of our happiness?

Shame

As I learn more and more about myself and my emotional states, I can start to recognise where my shame holds me in unhelpful repetitive patterns. As I now see these behaviours in a different way, shame starts to lose its meaning and opens up a new way of thinking about my emotions. Through honouring all my emotions, I can start to shift my shame.

I have already spoken a bit on vulnerability, but I would just like to say a few more words on shame. Shame is not just a sense of feeling embarrassed. To me, it is something deeper—a self-held belief on worthiness and ability, as I have already mentioned. Embarrassment may temporarily stop us or make us pause, but shame can paralyse us. When we feel shame, we are experiencing an internal belief system that tells us we are the embarrassment or guilt that we are feeling and have felt. Instead of seeing that embarrassment and guilt can assist us with navigating through life, we are in a position where we believe that those things are an integral part of who we are instead of being lessons from past experiences that we can learn from.

When I recognised the sources of my shame and what I was trying to cope with through the repetitive behaviours I created, I have found that my shame starts to become reframed. I start to see these past experiences and similar ones that I encounter now as opportunities for learning and engaging in new behaviours and routines that better serve me and who I want to be. Of course, we could have an entire book or even a series of books that look at shame in depth as it is a topic with much scope. What is important to take away from here, from my perspective, is that with some work, shame can be learned from and shifted in our lives. We can work on it on our own or with assistance and learn to reform our shame into something that works better for us. Of course, some people may need professional support, and my words are not meant to replace that. But maybe we can all take a bit of heart in knowing that shame does not have to be a fixed and static thing that forever inhibits us.

Stop, Swap, and Send

I have developed a tool for myself that I call stop, swap, and send that I would like to share with you. This is something that I developed to use when I am having unhelpful thoughts or reactions to things. When I remember to do this, it can make a difference in how I am being in the world at that time. I use it in situations where I unnecessarily react to things that occur in my life. It is a simple and straightforward tool that has been useful for me. It is also my belief that it can be helpful for others. If I start to think unhelpful thoughts and realise that maybe these thoughts are not serving me—I use stop, swap, and send.

I want to clarify here that this is not to be used to mask or ignore important emotions that can be difficult. If you are grieving a broken relationship, for example, or you have been affected by an experience that makes you angry, such as outrage over violence perpetrated against children, it is important to feel these emotions and to allow them to flow through you. What I am referring to are situations where you know your reaction could be different, but out of habit and conditioning, you have reacted in a way that is unhelpful.

A good example for me is when I get angry in the car when someone cuts me off. I know it is not helpful for me to have this anger and that it can affect my mood. I know that the person in the car may not have seen me as I may have been in their blind spot, or perhaps he or she was distracted by something that happened before getting in the car. In fact, it could have been anything. I know that there have been times I have cut people off and did not mean to. On the other hand, maybe the person in the car was driving aggressively and made an intentional move to make up time, get ahead, or whatever. For people like this, I also realise that I do not need to react badly, and I have realised that I can feel compassion for them. Either way, I do not know why these people are doing what they are doing. In my heart, I know that being compassionate is the way forward; for me, anyway.

Here is how it works.

I have been cut off, and I have used a number of expletives and maybe even thrown up my middle finger. During this I realise what I am doing and that it is unnecessary. So I use the first step: stop. I stop doing the actions that are unhelpful. If I am shaming myself for getting angry, I also stop that and allow myself to honour the fact that I did get angry, but now I am not. If it is helpful, I say to myself, "It is okay that I got angry. It is an old habit and does not serve me in this particular situation. I am not angry now, so I can stop this negative thinking." In the first part of this, I am literally using the word "stop" to assist me with stopping the behaviour and thinking, which I know is not serving me. I also use the word to generate awareness within me to avoid moving into a guilt or shame spiral around it.

After I have used stop, I then think, *Now it is time to swap.* What I do here is realise that I can swap what I am thinking and feeling for something that is more useful to me. In the example of the road rage, I usually need to swap my guilty, shameful thoughts to self-loving ones. Regarding the person I got angry with, I would swap my anger with compassion and love. I will formulate a statement along the lines of, "I love myself, and I feel happy and compassionate in this moment for both myself and this other person. We are both doing the best that we can on this drive in this moment." I repeat this to myself a few times and maybe even play with the language a bit until it feels right for me.

The next step is send. For some people, you may just use stop and swap, but I like to add send to the equation. With send I am taking the statement and feeling I have swapped and made an intentional movement to set it more fully into my consciousness and my present moment experience. I literally want to send my new energy out into the universe and into my heart. To help myself do this, I sometimes say to myself that I am sending this out with love. "I send compassion to myself and this other person with love in my heart and mind." To make this even more powerful, I say it out loud to myself. By saying it out loud I am making it into more of a reality for me in the present moment.

Another technique that I have used to make my affirmation more real for me is to say these things out loud to myself while looking into a mirror; maybe not doing this while driving, though. Saying affirmations while looking into a mirror can seem awkward at first, but with practice, it is a great way to start to develop self-love and self-compassion.

Exercise

Think of a time when you feel you may have unnecessarily gotten angry or frustrated. Now try applying stop, swap, and send in your imagination.

Imagine what it would be like to ask yourself to stop the thoughts and reactions you do not want to have.

Now imagine what you would like to swap those thoughts and reactions for. You can write this down or say it out loud to yourself.

Next, give send a try. Send this new thought out with love and compassion. You can either think it or say it as part of the new thought and emotion you want to have

Chapter 6

Realising Relationships

Change can also occur through developing awesome relationships.

In this section I explore how change can occur through developing a relationship with our self, with others, and with our community at large. I look at how, when we start to develop a relationship with ourselves, we create the opportunity to learn to take care of our physical, emotional, and spiritual well-being. Also, as we learn to nurture healthy relationships with others, we start to attract more of these types of supportive relationships into our lives. Then, through developing relationships with community, we see how great things can be accomplished together that are difficult to do alone.

It is my belief that change in the world occurs through initiating, nurturing, and retaining relationships. Relationships allow us to hold up a mirror to our lives in order to examine and reflect upon whom we are and the choices we have made for ourselves. I believe that change occurs through developing relationships with ourselves, with others, and with our community.

Relationship with Self

The first section is about having a relationship with yourself. Through developing a relationship with yourself, you learn to take care of your physical, emotional, and spiritual well-being. Developing a self-relationship is a form of self-care.

To put it simply, when we are healthy, we can help others be healthy. When we are happy, we can help others be happy. When we are awesome, we can spread the awesome. A brief example of this is that when parents take care of their own health, they are better able to take care of their children's health.

At this point, I think of the Dalai Lama and others like him. For instance, I have personally witnessed how when he enters a room and starts laughing, it is very difficult not to smile or even start laughing with him. I am sure we can all think of friends or family members with infectious behaviours who by being with us bring us into laughter, joy, or even love.

Part of having a relationship with yourself is about engaging in self-respect, self-acceptance and, self-compassion. Some of our inner talk can get in the way of those things we want to do or achieve. As we learn to respect, accept, and be compassionate with all of our emotions, behaviours, and thoughts, we can start to dissolve some of our inner barriers and experience the awesomeness within.

As infants and young children, the most important relationship we had was with our carers, be it a parent, grandparent, foster mother, and so on. These were the people who were supposed to keep us safe, feed us, love us, and provide us with the space to grow.

However, as adults, the most important relationship we can have is the one we nurture within; the one we have with ourselves. For a lot of people, this can be a difficult concept to grasp. But I do not believe it is that big of a leap for people to engage in this kind of thinking. We all know what it is like to self-gratify, to take care of ourselves, and to make choices that we feel are good for us. This is what I call taking care of yourself. Self-care definitely falls into this category for me.

I know that building a relationship with yourself may sound weird, but to me this is about exploring the question of who I am and actively engaging in self-respect, self-acceptance, and self-compassion. To say it in another way, self-respect is really a process of honouring myself.

I ultimately believe that we would see huge shifts around us in the world if more and more of us learned to love ourselves. Having a relationship with yourself does not necessarily have to involve self-love, but I cover more on self-love in a subsequent chapter.

Exercises

How would you describe your relationship with yourself?

How do you give yourself a hard time?

How do you respect, accept, and give compassion to yourself?

Self-Respect

Through having a relationship with myself, I have learned that I can respect myself. I can respect my emotions, respect my body, respect my intellect, and so on. When I start to respect myself more, I start to respect the world around me even more.

Self-respect helps to build our confidence and assists us with getting through difficult situations. When we respect ourselves, we are taking care of ourselves on many levels; we are taking care of our health, our emotional well-being, our minds, and our spirits. This also has a flow-on effect in that this then starts to show up as respect for others and our communities at large.

Self-respect does not have to be about having epiphanies or creating huge changes in our lives. It can be as straightforward as making a commitment to respecting yourself more. This can manifest as eating a piece of fruit a day or deciding to walk a flight of stairs occasionally instead of taking an elevator. Another example could be deciding to give ourselves a bit of a break when we have engaged in behaviours that we are ashamed of.

One powerfully awesome experience for me has been to learn to respect my emotions. For instance, respecting the anger I had around the car accident I described at the beginning of the book helped me to release the hold that incident had over my life. I used to refuse to be angry with the man who caused the accident because he died. I had an inner belief that because he died, I was being disrespectful by being angry. So I pushed this emotion down within me, but this did not do me any good. This, in part, fuelled unhelpful, angry responses to those close to me. When I realised that I was allowed to experience my anger and then gave myself permission to experience it, I was respecting that emotion and giving it space. It was unfortunate that this man died, and I still wish he had not, but through allowing myself to experience this anger towards him, I learned to be more compassionate with myself. Strangely enough, I felt a deeper compassion for this man I never met and the family he left behind.

Of course, to do some of these things on an ongoing basis takes practice along with an active choice to do things differently. We can assist this process through generating self-awareness and reframing the self-judgements we have from a place of self-love that does not involve the stories our egos can make for us.

Self-Acceptance

For me, part of this process is about learning to accept myself for who I am. When I am self-accepting, I am not judging myself. To me, a part of self-acceptance is learning from my experiences as well. It is not about denying what has happened. Rather, it is about releasing the unproductive emotional attachments I have attributed to them.

Sometimes it is the emotion I have around an experience that has prevented me from learning the lesson that particular experience had to teach me. As I self-accept, I can start to see my life in a different light. This continues with the process of honouring the self. Honouring the self is a big part of the relationship to self. When I am honouring who I am, I am more able to take responsibility for my actions, both the actions that I engage in with others and the actions that I engage in for myself.

Learning to honour ourselves is about accepting the whole of who we are. This may sound strange as often we think that we want to change or improve very specific things about ourselves. When we honour all these things, however, we can start to create the changes we may desire.

A good example of all this in action is accepting those times I have done things that have not been good for me, such as eating food that has been unhealthy for me on a continual basis. Through accepting that I have done this and not sitting in a place of guilt or shame over unhealthy eating habits, I can more easily make better eating choices for myself. I can look back and say that eating those unhealthy things gave me pleasure at the time, that they nourished me emotionally, but at the same time see that maybe eating all these things now does not serve me anymore. And with awareness, I can make changes that are good for me without feeling bad.

Self-Compassion

Another thing that occurs when I engage in a relationship with myself is that I start to be more compassionate with myself. I stop seeing myself as an object to be judged by me. Of course, I can still do things that I can learn lessons from, but now I know I can do this from a space of improving my life. I like to think of this in terms of cutting myself some slack. I personally find it easier to cut others some slack, but when I cut myself some slack, I relax quite a bit. There is a funny thing that happens when I cut myself some slack. I am also better able to be patient and understanding with others.

I can easily say that I have been my own worst enemy. I have often felt guilt or shame over things that I have done to others or that I have perceived I have done to others. When I make mistakes, I sometimes get angry with myself or frustrated at not "getting it right." I often create expectations for myself, and when I believe that I have not met those expectations, I beat myself up, metaphorically speaking, that is. Can you relate to this?

What I have learned, and I am still learning to put into practice, is that it is great to have expectations of myself.

However, I need to not be so concerned with outcomes. Sometimes experiences are out of my control, and other times I make choices out of habit. How I deal with outcomes, when I remember, is to look at them and learn, to accept that maybe things did not go my way and that it is okay that the results were different than what I expected. I have learned so much about myself from doing this. Approaching my experiences from a place of learning has allowed me to recognise both helpful and unhelpful patterns in my life and supported me in learning to honour my emotions.

I have seen how I have expanded my love, empathy, and compassion for others through practicing all these things within myself.

Building Relationships with Others

In this section I talk about the importance of building relationships with other individuals. Through nurturing relationships with other people, we can attract more positive and nurturing relationships into our lives and experience a greater sense of connectedness. When we do this we have an opportunity to express a wider range of emotional experiences, we are able to give and receive support, and through all of this, we have opportunities to grow and learn both separately and together.

Exercises

Please make a list of ten key relationships in your life.

Who in your life do you give support to?

Who in your life do you allow to give you support through challenging and/or difficult situations?

Shared Emotions

When we make it a priority to nurture relationships with other individuals, a large part of that involves emotional exchanges and reactions. Even if it is a colleague at work, you may share joys for a job well done, or you may get frustrated with each other, to name just two ways we could emotionally interact with others. In our more intimate relationships we can experience all sorts of emotional extremes. Often the more intimate or close we are to someone, the greater the depth of our feelings.

Our relationships allow us to engage in emotional exchanges where our old feeling patterns will be triggered, and new ones will arise. All of these can be explored and learned from as well if we want. With each new person in our lives, we are given a unique opportunity to explore our emotions, our behaviours, our patterns, and our reactions. To me, this is a wonderful way to experience a fuller range of who we are as each person will cause us to react in different ways. It is a truly awesome experience for us to be able to engage with others so that we can learn from them and learn how to navigate our emotional diversity and extremes.

If you have ever fallen in love with another person you will know how your experience of love can be enhanced by being with them. Love is a good example as people will write poetry, songs, make artwork, and do all sorts of things as they experience new expansions of their love. Other people give us an opportunity to express our love, and we give them opportunities to express it back to us.

Shared Support

As we get closer to other people, trust starts to build in the relationship. As this trust develops, we start to rely on others for support for whatever it is we are doing. To me, it is awesome to be able to get to a place with other people where they can support us in our endeavours, with our challenges, and with any difficulties we many encounter as we go through life. Not only do we have an opportunity to be supported ourselves, we also have the opportunity to support others. This is an awesome way for me to express my love and compassion in the world.

With other people's support, we can achieve great things, we can work out problems, and we can make it more easily through emotionally hard situations. It has been an extraordinary thing for me to learn that I do not always have to go it alone through difficult things.

In my business development, if it were not for the support of my wife, various friends, and my business coach, I would not be sitting and writing this book. They have provided support to me when I felt blocked in my writing or without structure. They have given me feedback on how to improve things, and they assisted me with the different emotions that have arisen in me through the process of writing. They have helped me overcome the emotions that initially came up for me about whether I was able to write, and they shared in the joy I have had with each stage of completion and success I have had in this awesomely wonderful process.

Shared Learning

As we share our emotions and our support with other people, we are also given an awesome opportunity for learning. Not only do we have the opportunity to learn new things about the world through our interactions with other people, but we also have the chance to learn much more about ourselves. When we are connected with others, they give us the opportunities to examine our thoughts, behaviours, and emotions. It is like others hold up a mirror to our lives that we can look into to get to know ourselves better.

When I have been frustrated with people I have worked with, for instance, and now look back at the experience, I can sometimes see how there is usually a trail of repetitive behaviours leading back in my life that are associated with my current frustration. Examining how I responded to the situation is a way for me to look at my life reflected back to me. But instead of seeing my face, I am observing my own emotions or thoughts.

Through observing my relationships with others from a compassionate basis, I have in part been able to learn how to be a better friend, a better husband, and a better family member. It is through my relationships with others that I have gained knowledge in how to have more nurturing and productive relationships in my life.

Building Relationships with Community

Exercise

How do you feel separate from the communities you are a part of?

How do you feel connected to the communities that you are a part of?

Through developing a relationship with community, I see how great things can be accomplished that are difficult to do alone. When I studied philosophy, I learned that Aristotle had the idea that "The whole is greater than the sum of its parts." Then when I was studying Gestalt psychotherapy, this theory underlined a good part of the teaching. In Gestalt, a number of theorists discussed this concept. People often attribute this to Wolfgang Kohler's or Kafka's writings as well, where they all said much similar things.

Without going into a long explanation of what this means from a philosophical or a psychotherapeutic way, I explain what it means to me in relation to being awesome and community. To put it in the most straightforward way I can think of, I see it as the idea that as a group we can create thoughts, structures, and systems that are bigger than all of us as individuals. So when we develop a relationship with community and move from self to other and then to many others, we have awesome opportunities to create wondrous things.

Here is one example of what I mean. On a straightforward level, two people who come together in love start to create a family unit that has meaning beyond just the pairing of a loving couple. The marriage of any two people has a significance that moves beyond the two individuals themselves. In fact, from my perspective, marriage is a part of community building, and this is one of many reasons why we need to open up the legal definitions of marriage to all people.

Another example I like to use is the Sydney Harbour Bridge. This was a structure built by the ideas, labour, and lives of many people. It is something that stands on its own above all the individuals who built it. It simply functions as a great bridge across an expansive harbour. It is more than that, though. It is also a symbol of Sydney and even Australia itself. It is a source of pride for Australians and something to be admired by visitors. In essence, it is something that is greater than the sum of all its parts. We can be like this in our relationships with community.

When we engage in a relationship with community, we also have the opportunity to expand our love with new ways and places to share it. An example of this for me is writing this book. Not only does it serve a purpose for myself, it is my hope that my words will assist some people. Even if they do not directly assist, maybe my words will start a conversation with some people around finding the awesome in their lives.

To me, this also goes back even further in my life. I feel that what has led me to this is the community of support and love I am immersed in. I also feel I have been supported by other people I have heard speak or who have written their own books or essays on life. I have been a community recipient of the wonderful teachings of people like the Dalai Lama, Sai Baba, the Hugging Mother, Louise Hay, and so on. I see all these people expanding community through expanding love.

The last thing I want to refer to with the concept of love and community is responsibility. I have seen how I have gained a greater responsibility for the world around me and how I am placed within it. I think it is awesome that when we build a relationship with community, we gain, learn, and earn a greater responsibility for the world around us. For me, this has expressed itself in a love for nature and respect for how important my interactions with it are. Through this I have learned that I am actually a part of nature, and it is a part of me. This heightens my responsibility. I think this is a wonderfully extraordinary idea.

Relationship Exercise

At this time, I want you to think about and write down one way that you can nurture your relationship with yourself. An example for me is doing mirror work, where I have affirmations on my mirror at home to remind me to tell myself that I love myself. I then look at myself in the mirror and say these words.

Now, write down one way that you can nurture a relationship with another person in your life. One thing that I have done is try to remember to say thank you to my wife at least once a day for something she has done. Sometimes it may not happen, but often it does. The intent and action of love goes a long way.

Lastly, try and think of a way that you can engage in nurturing your relationship with one of the communities you may be associated with. One way I do this is to travel into Sydney from where I live to attend social gatherings with close friends. Another example is that in the past, I have been involved in certain social justice and environmental movements as well.

Chapter 7

Love

As I learn how to feel and express love in new and different ways, I also learn how love assists me in creating an awesome and extraordinary ongoing experience of contentment, clarity, and fulfilment.

As we start to refine—or in some cases acquire—the skills of how to truly love ourselves, how to love others unconditionally, and how to express our love to all things, we can discover a personal fullness in our lives that makes us realise that we, too, can be awesome. When we nurture our self-love, we feel more relaxed and peaceful. This makes it easier for us to make the healthy and productive choices that we want to make for ourselves.

Through expressing love to others and feeling love from them, we feel a heightened sense of connection that provides us with the opportunity to learn more about ourselves. Then through expressing our love to all things, we learn that we have a connection to all things. It is this love that creates these connections. All of these expressions of love assist us in seeing how we can attract things into our lives that are positive and in alignment with how we want to live.

This chapter is about exploring just a few dimensions of the many aspects of love. I have lots of beliefs and concepts about love and what it means to me. This is another topic on which many books, poems, songs, and movies have been the focussed. In fact, many explorations of love will continue to be produced. How could this not be the case? For the purpose of this chapter, though, I only discuss love and what it means from my perspective in relation to having an awesome and extraordinary life with and for yourself, others, and community. Who knows; maybe one day I will write a book about love as it is so beautifully rich and pervasive.

In some ways, this chapter is really an extension of the last chapter. I suggest that when we explore love through relationship and connectedness, we can go even deeper into our understanding of self and other. I feel that love is actually like a type of glue that connects us all. When we learn to express more love to and from ourselves, others, and community, we have the opportunity to learn, grow, and change in ways that are productive and beneficial to us all.

When I live from love, I have seen awesome things happen. I have witnessed how it can melt an argument, how it can overcome adversity, and how it can transform a tense situation into a memorable one. To me, living from the present also means living from love.

Exercises

What is love to you?

When you think of love, who or what do you do you think of?

Write down a story of when kindness or love made a difference in your life.

What Does Love Mean to Me?

In brief, love to me is the all-connecting emotion. From my perspective, it is the feeling that leads me into and through my spirituality. In previous chapters I have spoken about how it is important for us to experience all our emotions, and, of course, this includes love. From my personal experience, I have discovered that I can link love to all my emotions, even anger. I have learned that sometimes when I have been angry, it is because I felt a love for something, or when I approach my anger with love, I can gain learning for myself.

To me, love is something that comes from within. It is not something to be obtained; much like my views that I shared on happiness. We often believe that we need to find or get something or someone in order to find love. The idea that love is a thing to be found is a way of objectifying something that is actually already within us. Love is found within everyone. It is one of the things that assist us with navigating the highs and lows of our lives.

As I explore love in my life, I feel more whole within myself, and awesome things happen for me. Love is like a conduit for a deeper learning and understanding of myself and the world in which I live. Through love I gain contentment, clarity, and fulfilment.

Love Yourself Like There Is No Tomorrow

When I nurture my self-love, I feel more relaxed and peaceful in my life, making it easier for me to make the choices that I want to make for myself. Self-love is about enhancing my relationship with myself and allowing myself to feel and express love independently of others.

Self-love is a very important part of much of what I have been sharing in this book. I have been pointing at this throughout the book, recognising the role I play in perpetuating repetitive behaviours, honouring my emotions, and engaging in a relationship with myself. You have probably already noticed that a lot of the ideas I have been talking about are intertwined with each other, just like in the whole of our lives we are complex, interwoven beings where no one part of us or our lives truly stands alone.

Self-love is also about being compassionate with myself for mistakes I may have made or behaviours that I am not particularly proud of. Self-love makes it easier to love other people as well, for once I start to love myself, it is easier to express this to others.

Self-Nurturing

Focusing on yourself can be very important. Learning to nurture ourselves can have many benefits for us. It enhances the relationship with self that we have developed and strengthens our coping capacity, our health, and our mental, emotional, and spiritual growth. Self-care can truly be an act of loving ourselves.

I have grown up in a world that equates self-care and choices made for your own benefit as being selfish and as a negative thing. Hence, the idea of self-care becomes muddled into the definition of being selfish. Cheryl Richardson's book *Extreme Self-Care* is a good start on looking at a different way of being concerned with self. From my perspective, if I am physically, emotionally, and mentally taken care of, I can better support others. Being stoic does not always serve us and can, in fact, be disruptive to our lives. There may be times when being stoic is helpful in terms of dealing with a difficult situation, but in day-to-day life, it often leads us to push down and ignore those emotions that are so important for us to feel.

Me time is important for me. When I give myself time to look after myself, I am better able to connect with others and be productive. My me time is the space I take in my life for self-care, unwinding, relaxing, and rejuvenating myself. A personal example of some simple me time is unwinding by reading a science fiction or fantasy fiction novel at the end of the day or watching some of my favourite movies or television programs. Other types of me time I engage in are when I take the time for activities such as exercise and meditation.

Another example of some self-care behaviours is recognising when I need to say no to people and situations. A healthy boundary can result in taking care of ourselves and of showing ourselves that we are concerned not just about the consequences of actions on others but of also on ourselves. Sometimes, of course, it can be a great learning experience for us to enter into a challenge, such as setting a healthy boundary. But this can be a type of me time when we do it with awareness. On the other side, though, we may know that if we enter into a situation that may trigger us or take lots of our energy, we may choose to avoid it as we know this particular situation may not serve as well as we want it to. We can awesomely choose how to engage in our self-focus.

Sometimes we can be our own worst enemies. As I have outlined before, we can be cruel to ourselves and not very forgiving. But we can also create the circumstances for this to be different. When we apply love to ourselves, we gain an internal empathy and compassion that is inwardly focused. This inward focus of love and compassion can assist us in calming our minds, being more in the present moment, and gaining awareness of our own thinking and actions. With love we learn to forgive ourselves so that we can experience the wonderful and awesome effect of inner peacefulness. The act of learning to self-love and then to forgive ourselves is, to me, one of the most truly extraordinary gifts we can give to ourselves. I write a bit more on forgiveness later in the book.

When we engage in nurturing and loving ourselves, we are being compassionate, gentle, kind, forgiving, and nonjudgemental towards ourselves. When we do this for ourselves, this also provides us with a good foundation to be loving and compassionate to others.

Exercise

What are some ways that you already engage in self-love?

List some new ways that you could engage in self-love that you have not previously practiced. This could be as simple as patting yourself on the back for a job/task well done.

Love Love's Company

Through expressing our love to others and feeling love from them, we feel a heightened sense of connection with them. Love most definitely strengthens our relationships, and through this, we also get an opportunity to learn more about ourselves.

Continuing on from my theme of building relationships with others, I feel that when we share our love with others, great things can happen for us. The inner awesome can really start to be exposed when we share our love. When I share my love and others share their love with me, it is the most amazing thing. Think about how good it has felt to have shared love with people you love as well. It is a truly wondrous thing to me. We can see how books, poetry, songs, art, marvels of architecture, and much more have all been created in the name of love. How can we not have awesomeness without love?

I would like to say that I am being very intentional with using the word "share" in regards to love. Love is something that is natural and surrounds all of us. We all have the capacity to be in touch with it and to share it with others and the world at large. When we share love, we are not only recognising the innate love within ourselves but also acknowledging and honouring the innate love that exists within others.

For me, this is an important distinction from giving our love to others. There are acts of giving that are appropriate, of course, and we traditionally think of what we do around love as giving, and for some people, part of that is about giving the love freely. I like to reframe the idea of giving into one of sharing as from my experiences, I have observed that love is a natural process. I have realised that I have never ever actually given my love away. When I reflect upon how and when I have shared my love, as opposed to when I thought I have given my love away, I realise that it is still within me. So in a sense, from my perspective anyway, it makes more sense to see it as a sharing. When I meditate on this, it feels warmer to me to think of sharing love as love is ultimately a connecting force between people.

When I am sharing my love, I observe that it is not actually being received by the other. This could also be seen as objectifying it as well. Rather, it is connecting with the love the other person has within him or her. To me, the act of sharing is an act of activating the awareness of love in the other person; the love this person already naturally has within him or her. When this happens, the actual sharing that occurs is a mutual expression and feeling of love. As I share my love with you and you share it with me, we are activating it in each other. For me, the idea of sharing love with the other is a very beautiful idea.

On a different level, when we share our love, we are also acknowledging our own self-love and the love we may have for that which is greater than us. We essentially are vessels for sharing love. Through our actions, we become both the manifestation and conduit of love.

When I really think about the phrase, "giving my love," it does not seem quite right—particularly in the context of what I have just shared. The reason for this is that the act of giving, for me, invokes the thought of an object, something separate and apart from the self and even the other. Giving sets love up as a thing that can be parted with. The idea of giving also makes me start to think of love as a possession, which does not seem correct to me. When I am actually feeling love, it does not feel like a possession. It feels like something that is just a part of me, emanating from me, and connecting with the love that is emanating from another. Maybe this is just splitting hairs, but this seems to make love something even more sacred to me. Maybe this idea works for you as well.

Exercise

I would like you to think of a time when you felt love for someone else. It might help to quiet your mind as though you are doing a meditation, get grounded, and invoke the memory of your loving experience. Explore the thoughts, feelings, and even body sensations that you may have associated with that experience. Does it feel like giving or sharing to you? Of course, there is no right or wrong here as giving love freely is a wonderful concept. But maybe this idea of sharing is something that will resonate with you.

All of this does not mean to say I cannot give someone a symbol of my love. When I do, I am not giving my love away. Rather, I am creating symbolism around the love that is still within me, that I am sharing, and that I recognise within the other as well. Symbolism can be quite significant in regards to love. Through symbolism, we are reminded that the love is already within us and is also eternal. When we have trouble connecting with our love, this symbolism from another can be the catalyst that reminds us that love is within.

I am still adopting the concept of sharing myself, and I am still catching myself using the word "give." But when I get down to it, I am really talking about sharing. As I learn to love myself and share it with others, I have witnessed how it has transformed relationships for me. When I have felt bad or judgemental about others and apply the idea of sharing my love with them, I have noticed how these relationships soften and get easier. I do not even have to say, "I love you," to them or that I am sharing my love with them. Just through saying it to myself and expressing it in my actions I have seen great changes.

As I engage in sharing love and acknowledging this connection of love with others and within myself, I have observed that there is also an extraordinary process of cause and effect in relationships. If I am loving, compassionate, and understanding, I often notice that there is an immediate effect on how I feel about certain situations, and as I just mentioned, the relationships I have with others somehow become much easier to navigate. The cause of my love and compassion being expressed has an effect on those around me.

Life Is Love, so Let Us Love Life

Through expressing my love to all things, I learn that I have a connection to all things. I see how I can attract things into my life that are positive and align with how I want to live. I have learned that when I am present and aware, I can see and experience love everywhere as love is a part of me and a part of everyone. Then when I see that love is everywhere, I see just how awesome life is all around me. Seeing the love is seeing the awesome in all of us and in the world. When we learn to love ourselves, when we learn to love others, and when we learn to express our love to all things, we can find contentment, fulfilment, and clarity.

Exercise

What I would like to do right now is ask you to engage in an exercise of your imagination. Imagine what your life would be like if everything was connected by and through love.

I used to not believe that we were surrounded by love. But through imagining it, I have seen how it has transformed my life. Even if we were to pretend that life is love, imagine how awesome that would be. If we acted like all of life was love—and everyone acted like all of life was love—imagine how awesome this would be. Everything would become much more sacred. We now know that the brain sometimes cannot distinguish between reality and imagination on an emotional level. So as we start to imagine love everywhere, we can actually start to feel it, and see the changes around us the more we do this.

I say let us play with the idea that all of life is love. If we act like all of life is love, why can't we all be infinitely awesome and extraordinary?

Inspires Compassion in Community

Part of the sharing of love to me is about generating empathy and compassion. We could not have healthy, functioning communities without empathy and compassion for others. These are some of the building blocks of community. Part of the fabric of our societies is a mutual understanding grounded in these things. We learn to respect others through our understanding of love. As we express our love to community, we can create awesome societies.

On a small scale, this starts within the home; the society of family, so to speak. When parents care for children, this comes from love and understanding the needs they have. Our innate sense of empathy that gets generated through love helps us to understand these needs. We can apply this model of understanding that we naturally generate through family in expressions of love to our communities, moving from one structure to the other.

When we start to share our love with community, we gain respect not just for the people we know but also for other people we meet. When we see tragedy in the news or know that others are experiencing hardship, our love for community can lead us and others to support those in need of assistance and support. When we add love to the concept that we can create things grander than the sum total of their parts, we end up with compassionate and dynamic structures that can serve our societies and the world at large.

Chapter 8

Celebration

Engaging in celebration honours achievements,
opens up the opportunity for further creativity,
and cultivates community.

When we engage in celebrations, we cultivate our relationships and communities and honour our own achievements and those of others. These things can also be an awesome way of capturing and expressing our creativity. Celebration is important as it connects us to what we have achieved. It also provides us with the opportunity to connect with others and what they have accomplished in their lives. Through honouring our achievements, we are expressing our self-love. Through honouring other people's achievements, we are given an opportunity to share love with others. Celebrating also provides us with the circumstances for not only honouring creativity but also a way of expressing it at the same time. When we celebrate, we are expressing the personal power we derive from acknowledging and living from the present moment.

I have discovered how important it is to engage in celebration as it honours my personal achievements and those of others. It opens up the opportunity for myself and others to further explore our creativity and provides circumstances for us to cultivate our communities. Celebration also assists me in renewing my energy and providing me with inspiration and motivation.

Exercise

What do you celebrate about yourself?

What do you celebrate within the communities that you are a part of?

The more I move through my life, the more I realise that celebration has a larger role to play than I once thought. When I was younger, celebration was something for birthdays, Christmas, Thanksgiving, graduations, and so forth. Of course, these are still celebrations to me, but I have learned from them how celebration can have a wider scope that is of benefit to the way I lead my life. Celebrations can be ritual, or ceremonies, or standalone events and experiences.

Ceremony is an important part of what we all do. If we really want to break it down, we could look at all of our behaviours, responses, and actions as ceremonies. We ritualise many of the things that we do in our lives. I, for one, have a morning routine that works well for me and usually assists me with getting a good start into my day. From my perspective, this is a ritual and ceremony, so to speak. If we go back to the earlier chapters on repetitive behaviours and honouring emotions, we can start to see those processes in a new light when we look at them from a perspective of celebration. If my behaviours are rituals/ceremonies and I am honouring the behaviours and the emotional and intellectual responses implicit within them, a natural next step for me is to see them as celebrations. I have learned that when I look at things from this perspective, I can bring love into many aspects of my life.

I want to make it clear that I am not saying that we engage in a reductionist view of celebration and boil it all down into an emotional melting pot where celebration becomes commonplace and, hence, loses its meaning as something special. What I am suggesting is that when we apply the idea of celebration to things that we do, we can gain a new appreciation and gratitude for those things in our lives that we engage in and are important even if they are routine. In other words, we increase our awareness of the importance of even simple and straightforward actions that we engage in that keep us going on a daily basis. I suggest we try to imagine what it would be like if we looked at all our actions as celebrations of who we are, what we do, and life in general. When I do this, I find that my life feels much richer and fuller. When I have love and gratitude for many things, my life gets easier and more fulfilling to me. You see, when I look at my life through the lens of honouring emotions, love, and celebration, I see I am honouring myself as a whole and honouring life as a whole as well.

At the same time, though, it is also important to have celebration as something special that stands out. This type of celebration also has a big role to play in our lives, especially in relation to our achievements.

Honouring Achievements

Through celebrating my own achievements, I honour my accomplishments. This gives me an opportunity to express my own love to self. Through celebrating other people's achievements, I am also given an opportunity to honour their accomplishments and share love with them.

Celebration is important as it connects me to what I have achieved. It provides me with opportunities to connect with others and what they have accomplished in their lives. Celebration also provides me with the circumstances for not only honouring creativity but also with a way of expressing it at the same time.

When we engage in celebrations, we cultivate relationships and communities and, thus, honour our achievements and those of others. When we do this, these things can be an awesome way of capturing and expressing our creativity as well.

When I celebrate, it provides me with an opportunity to build my relationship with myself and to engage in self-love. I am learning in my life how to create these acknowledgements for myself in order to honour within myself what I have accomplished. Sometimes I manifest this in the simplest ways. One example that I would like to share is that upon completion of one significant segment of writing for this book, I celebrated by taking myself out to an awesome cafe in Katoomba, a town near where I live, for a great coffee and meal. This was a simple and straightforward way for me to honour something I had achieved that was important to me. Sometimes I do things that are bigger to celebrate, but sometimes the action only needs to be modest. What is important is that I did something out of the ordinary in self-acknowledgement.

Celebrations also provide me with an opportunity to build relationships with others and to share my love with them. When I invite others to celebrate my achievements with me, I feel fully connected with them. We have fun and enjoy each other's company all built around acknowledging something in my life.

Celebrating achievements in my life has not always been an easy thing for me to do. Inviting others to join me in celebrating something I have accomplished used to seem overwhelming or arrogant to me. I needed to get over the self-critic within me that said I did not deserve such things. I have learned that this was the part of me that sometimes felt awkward at being the centre of attention. Sometimes these thoughts still arise, but the difference now is that I am aware of them. I can let my sense of feeling or being unworthy come and go and then realise and own that it is okay to celebrate my own achievements. In other words, my awareness of my thoughts around celebrating things for myself has allowed me to express compassion and love to myself. Then when I invite others in, I provide them with the opportunities to share their love, to make their connections, and to interact with each other and me in our own personal ways that allow for relationships to grow.

When I engage in celebrating the achievements of others with them, I also see the same opportunities as I just described. I see opportunities to honour my friends and family in the things that they have achieved. I am given the chance to connect with them and to share the love I feel for them from my perspective.

I find it a truly awesome and wonderful thing to join others in celebrating their lives. In fact, this also provides me with the opportunity to celebrate my life. When I am celebrating with others, I am given the space to express myself, to experience things in the present moment, to feel my emotions as they arise, and to be able to share my love with others.

Creativity

As I have mentioned, celebration also provides us with the circumstances for not only honouring our creativity but also with a way of expressing it at the same time. Our personal celebrations and the celebrations for others create the opportunity for us to engage in new behaviours and experiences. In other words, these experiences create the opportunity for us to be creative within ourselves and with other people. We can create new rituals and ceremonies, and we can create new ways of being in the world through our acts of celebration.

Celebration is also one big, awesome act of creativity. On a straightforward level, I can be creative with inventing my own celebrations, how it plays out, and what I am going to do. In regards to others, if I am asked to assist in creating an event, I am also given an opportunity to be awesome and engage in creativity. When we have celebrations, we are truly manifesting our lives. We have an intention that develops into an idea, and that leads to the creation of actions and, ultimately, ends up in an event that is both tangible and new.

Now we can take this last idea and apply it to everything that we choose to do. When we are in awareness and choose to do something, we create our lives and our reality. Celebration helps me realise that I can create all aspects of my life or at least all my reactions to what has happened in my life.

Another aspect of celebration that is truly awesome to me is that even if I have not been part of the planning of an occasion, I am still a part of the manifesting of it by participating. I play a role in creating a wonderful reality in connection with those around me.

The space of celebration can also inspire me. When I have been to celebrations, I often go away feeling inspired to create new things in my life, to create the changes I want to make, and to create the person I aspire to be. I can see and experience something that is new and creative, and this inspires new thoughts, plans, and actions for me to play with and try out in my life. To me, it is a wonderful and awesome thing to be inspired by others to create new things around me. When I think about these processes of inspiration and creativity, I realise just how truly we are interconnected beings. I find it extraordinary that I can be inspired through the act of celebration.

Another part of being inspired is that this feeds my mind, my spirit, and even my body. Often when I have been inspired into creativity, I feel a rejuvenation within me that touches all of these things. I get a renewed energy. I find this very interesting because when this happens for me, it is like an internal transformation has occurred within. When my creative spirit is awakened, any mental, emotional, or physical fatigue I have been experiencing will often just melt away and be replaced by a new vitality. To my thinking, this must be because I am connecting to love and letting the energy of all life that I am connected to flow through me.

Community

When we engage in celebrations, we cultivate and nurture our relationships and communities. As we honour our own achievements and those of others, we build and strengthen the foundations of our community structures.

Celebration has a lot of significance in our world. On a societal and cultural level, it will sometimes mark the end of something adverse, such as celebrating the end of the two world wars of the twentieth century. At other times, celebration is used to mark an achievement such as Canada Day to mark the founding of the country in 1867. Within the world's various religious and spiritual structures, there are many revered days that are ritualised and celebrated. These types of celebrations are a big part of our communities. They are things that we share with friends and family, and they can sometimes be the glue that holds our communities together. Sometimes these celebrations of common purpose provide the energy and rejuvenation we need to move through our lives.

When we engage in celebrating with others, we not only engage in building relationships with each other and sharing our love but often move these things into the realm of something that is larger than us. I feel we are actually building community in these spaces. We are engaging in the spiritual connection that moves us all beyond the self and even the interpersonal interactions between just a few people.

A celebration can often feel larger than life. How many times have we heard, "larger than life"? For me, a great example of "larger than life" is the type of celebration we have around a wedding. A wedding is a great example of how the whole will often feel greater than the sum of its parts. In the wedding we are engaging our spirits, we are linking into each other's love, and celebrating the love of the people who are making public their vows of love for each other. We can feel like we are linking into those concepts of life that seem not only to be a part of us but to also be greater or larger than us.

With a wedding we have an awesome opportunity to witness and be a part of the opening up and experiencing of love not just between two people or even between two families but also across our communities. Weddings seem to move beyond the event and ceremony itself and out into the world at large. It is not only a transition time for the couple involved, where they are declaring their love and partnership to the world, it also creates a transition in the world itself as our communities now see them in the light of a publicly celebrated union.

The writing of this book is a big celebration of who I am. In the writing of it, I am honouring myself and those who helped me get to where I am today. Writing this book has also created the circumstances for me to be creative with my thinking and share it with you. In the process of writing, I have been able to connect with many people who assisted me and, hopefully, on some level with you the reader as well. Writing the book has, of course, been a lot of work, but it has also been a celebration of where I have come to in my life. Built into the book journey for me, as I have mentioned, have been a number of smaller celebrations with a few more to come, including a big one or two to mark the completion of the book and final edits.

To end this chapter, I acknowledge that celebration is a part of an awesome and amazing process that can be expressed in a multitude of ways. It is way of marking endings and beginnings. But at the same time, it is neither the end nor the beginning. Through celebration we honour ourselves and others, we create, and we connect. Let us all celebrate each other and our own selves.

Exercise

Think of at least five new ways you can engage in celebration in your life either for yourself or others.

Chapter 9

Forgiveness

I have learned and experienced how forgiveness can set me free.

Through having my own experience of learning to forgive others, I have seen that forgiveness is like a balm that only I can apply to myself. Forgiveness to myself from myself is also a part of this process. I have learned that we can be our own worst enemy in the forgiveness process. When we learn to accept the past as the past and learn from it, we can free ourselves of repetitive thoughts and emotions in the present that may not be serving us. When we have done this we can then start connecting with others and share the self-love that arises within us as we let go of those things that bind us.

Exercise

What does forgiveness mean to you?

How do you engage in the process of forgiveness?

Forgiveness Frees Me

So what does forgiveness mean to me? I will try to explain.

As a child growing up, forgiveness, as I learned it, was a process that we did for someone else. If someone did something to us that we did not like, we learned to forgive him or her because we cared about the person and wanted to continue to do so. I also learned the expression, "Time heals all," and to a certain degree, I have seen how some time and some space from a painful experience can assist us in gaining a new perspective. I learned to forgive in this way when I felt transgressed against but still wanted to be connected to the transgressor.

Forgiveness was something that was to be given or granted to another person. On the other hand, I was also taught to seek forgiveness when I had wronged people and to ask someone to forgive me if I had done some wrong towards him or her. So forgiveness, as I used to understand it, was something to be received or given, an emotional object that was dependent on the magnanimity of me and or someone else.

What I want to suggest is that we can alter this view of forgiveness. I would like to suggest that forgiveness is something that we do to ourselves. That the starting place of forgiveness towards others begins with forgiving ourselves. I am suggesting that forgiveness, much like how I have discussed love, is something that comes from within and can be shared as opposed to being given away. Forgiveness is a journey that starts within so that we can free ourselves from being caught up in repetitive thoughts and emotions that are based on past experiences.

I have observed that sometimes even when I have received a real and heartfelt apology from those I feel wronged me, I do not always feel better. This used to feel strange to me. I would remain angry and frustrated. I would live in the woundedness that was created within me as my reaction to the experience. I have learned that when I looked at how feeling angry, frustrated, and wounded have repeated themselves in my life, they no longer serve me in relationships. I have seen that, for me, what my hurt is covering up is my own wounded pride. I have learned that when I am feeling this emotional pain again and again, they are old ideas, experiences, interpretations, and beliefs that I am still attached to now in the present moment. To me, there is an irony in this as my attachment to the past can make it difficult for me to get grounded in the present.

Part of this learning for me is that I believed the other person was supposed to be a certain way, but he or she did not live up to what I created in my mind. I learned that some of my pain was created from thinking that others should behave in a specific way that lived up to what my expectations of them were. Well, as we know, this does not always happen. Others simply do not behave according to how we believe they should behave—as much as we may wish them to. On some intellectual level, I have known this since being young, but the difference for me is that when things get tough or do not go our way, I will sometimes forget that others do not always do what I may expect them to do. To truly learn this lesson, I needed to have an experience of this that touched me emotionally as well as intellectually.

Forgiveness is about allowing ourselves to be freed from the negative emotions that can trap us when we feel we have been wronged or violated in some way. When I look at experiences where I have felt wronged, I have come to realise these are things from my past that live in my memory. I have learned that I can now choose how to interpret these past experiences in the present moment. I can either stay wounded or recognise that this past experience no longer has to have an influence over me in the present. This can take time for some people. I know that it does for me, but I am getting better at finding my personal power in the present moment in relation to those past, emotionally difficult experiences.

Sometimes in the forgiveness process we can be our own worst enemies. Not forgiving ourselves can be a tricky and slippery thing. It can get in the way of having a satisfying and awesome life. The more we learn to forgive ourselves, the easier it gets to live a happy, fulfilling, and awesome life.

Forgiveness towards myself does not always come easily for me. Nor does learning how to express my forgiveness towards others after I have forgiven myself. What does help, though, is remembering that this is an approach that works for me, and I have seen and experienced how it can make a difference in my life. What also helps is when I remember that part of the key to this is allowing myself to self-love.

Forgiveness is something that I am still learning to practice in my life. When I talk about self-forgiveness, I am referring to being loving and compassionate to yourself around your own thoughts and feelings. I used to beat myself up over getting so easily triggered back to those negative emotions I have had around experiences where I felt wounded. I would get frustrated with myself and say things like, "Sebastian, why do you keep doing that." This changed for me when I started to honour all of my emotions—the anger, the frustration, love, and so on. When I started to do this, my layer of self-anger and frustration started to erode and disappear. It can still be with me and gets triggered, but now I recognise what it is and move on, even if it takes me some time to remember to do this. By the way, this also helps with the anxiety I have, which I mentioned earlier in the book.

I have noticed that when I have forgiven myself, it is so much easier to forgive others. For me it feels like an extension of the love that I want to share with them.

I want to make it clear, though, that I am not saying when we forgive we are excusing all behaviours we deem unacceptable. Forgiveness is not about forgetting certain wrongs that have been committed wilfully or otherwise. We all learn to some degree through getting stuff wrong, forgiving ourselves, sharing this with others, and moving on. Part of forgiveness is about learning from mistakes and errors. It also helps us set up the mutually agreed rules of our communities in order for us to move on and interact in ways that make sense to us. It is helpful in intimate relationships so that we can navigate through all sorts of challenging times. Forgiveness in the case of wrongs committed can be a type of learning for interaction with others but can also be a type of learning and accepting our own inner strength and love.

When I forgive myself for holding onto unhelpful emotions, I start to free myself. When this happens, I can share my love more freely with myself and others. It strengthens connections and can assist with building compassionate communities. When my love is free from being bound by my lack of forgiveness, I can feel how love is actually boundless, and it is only I who am holding it back.

What is important for me here is intention. When we sit with an intention and act on it, we can start to affect change. Forgiveness for me cannot be forced, I have discovered. What seems to work for me is to have the intent and to try and remember to avoid giving myself a hard time. If I do give myself a hard time, I can recognise it as being unhelpful and then shift my feelings. When my thoughts are focused around this and I am engaging in love for self and others or even community, the easier it gets for me to forgive. I have learned that forgiveness is a dynamic process that sometimes comes easily and sometimes takes time. But I have learned that I can forgive others and myself even for things that seemed really huge at the time of the initial experience.

The Balm We Can Self-Apply

When we look at forgiveness as something that comes from the self for the self, we can start to see our emotions in a different light. When we do this, we start to take responsibility for our own emotions. As we take responsibility for our emotions, we start to realise the power that we have within ourselves.

What is amazing to me is that when I start to take responsibility for how I respond to a past experience, it often has an impact on the other people in my life—including, of course, the person I was seeing as a transgressor. I will notice that there is lightness in my being, which makes it easier for me to engage people and build or rebuild important relationships. I can honestly say that having been through these forgiveness processes that I have been able to feel better about myself and have better relationships with others.

Now, of course, forgiveness can be difficult. I have struggled with it myself as I have mentioned. I have realised that it is something for me to do within myself, and it is not the other person who is creating the continual suffering that I have felt over certain past experiences. At the same time, this awareness has not always felt like enough. For me, it has been a process of intentions and insights. When I have set these intentions and been loving towards myself, it has made it easier.

Within this framework I have used forgiveness in the forgiveness process itself. What I mean is that I have cut myself some slack when I have fallen into resentment or anger towards the person I believed wronged me. I have learned to apply a balm of self-forgiveness to my own struggle to forgive. There have been times I have fallen into my resentment or anger and then been upset with myself for not living up to my self-imposed expectations. But I have learned that I can forgive myself for going into that space and to let go of those strong emotions that can hold me trapped in my own past.

As we know, forgiveness can be a tricky thing. The societal framework around how it plays out can be strong and vary from culture to culture. I truly believe, though, that part of the key lies within each and every one of us in the choices we make for ourselves. This does not mean we have to deny our cultural references. Rather, from my perspective, it is something that can add to them.

Remember: Forgiveness Is Free

I know saying that forgiveness is free is self-apparent. The reason I say it, though, is to remind myself that like love, it is something that exists within me that I can open myself up to. It is something that can assist me with having an awesome life. As forgiveness is free, I can share it with others and myself, thus allowing me to express my love and compassion more fully both externally and internally.

Pulling Forgiveness Together

I would like to use forgiveness as an example of how I put being present, recognising my behaviours, honouring emotions, realising relationships, expressing love, and using celebration together to create change for me. Of course, any part of these things can make a difference and, in fact, have.

But I want to show how they can work together and have done so for me.

As an example of how I have done this I would like to share an experience I went through regarding forgiveness and my grandfather. When I was around maybe twenty years old, I learned some things that my grandfather did to my mother when she was younger. The details are not important, but it was enough to make me upset with him. Prior to this I held an anger towards him as a result of how he drastically changed the way he treated me when I turned into a teenager. Remember, I mentioned that I can be highly sensitive, and put that on top of the loyalty I feel for my parents and brother, I developed quite a resentment.

When I learned about how he had treated my mother, I became angry with him, building on the old resentment I had silently harboured for years over his changed behaviour towards me and that I had not yet dealt with. So for a number of years, I was unable to forgive him. The funny thing is I do not think he even knew I had these feelings. It was something I only shared with a couple of people.

A few years later, while I was travelling, I found it within me to begin to forgive him. More recently, I was able to enter into an even fuller feeling of forgiveness around him, a feeling that was more about my well-being and the well-being of those around me who would hear my thoughts about what he had done. I would like to use my insights to describe parts of the processes that I believe were at play throughout this for me.

When I look back, I can see how one thing that I did was start to enhance my awareness in the present moment, learning in the process how I was letting those thoughts negatively influence my life. At the time, I started to see that things could be different for me in relation to my grandfather. As a result, I almost immediately started to feel more connected with the present moment, and this made a difference to even my day-to-day life at the time.

I was travelling in India at the time and had inadvertently started to follow a path there learning about meditation, how to cultivate my awareness. and live from the present moment; things that I am still doing. Through this I began to see a few things about what was going on for me. One was that this was an experience that happened in the past.

I also realised that what I needed to do was give myself a break, to let these things remain in the past, and to learn from them in the present moment. I used to beat myself up mentally over how I felt about my grandfather. After I stopped doing that and forgave myself for having these negative feelings, I was able to more fully experience all my emotions I had around my grandfather.

I became aware that the experience my mother had was not mine to take on board, and this made a difference for me. I realised that I had taken on my own interpretations of my mother's experiences even though they were hers to contend with. What I am referring to here is how we can sometimes make ourselves responsible for things that others do or have had done to them. This is good in the case of a parent protecting a child and so forth. However, it can be inhibiting when we take on other people's experiences as our own.

The other realisation was that the experience I had with my grandfather was in the past, and we actually had a good relationship again now that I was older. I had not acknowledged that feeling within me, and when I did take ownership of the fact I resented him in the past but that we were getting along really well at that time, I started to feel liberated. My repetitive pattern in my head of making him wrong for his actions was broken within me. I could see it as an unhelpful behaviour that was no longer serving me. The hurt I had at spending less time with him as a child had turned into a habit of avoiding him or complaining to my mother. This was my creative way of protecting myself as a teenager. With my new awareness, I realised that I no longer needed to be this way as an adult.

At the same time, I started to recognise my own emotions in relation to what happened. I learned to honour and respect them. It was okay that I felt hurt by him acting differently towards me for a short time in my life. And it was okay that I felt those things around my mother as I love and care about her. But at the same time as doing this, I freed my emotions up enough that I started to get in touch with my love for my grandfather. I have great memories of us doing things together when I was a child. He also treated me well as I got a bit older. When I warmed to these things and accepted them, I felt things shift within me.

I also started to see that I had a repetitive behaviour of nonforgiveness for other things in my life as well. My new awareness of my repetitive behaviours helped me to see how I have done this in friendships and relationships as well in the past. This made me realise that I did not always have to repeat this unhelpful and reactive process.

Having these realisations let me see how I was holding myself back in relationships I was having. I would hold onto resentments or frustrations I had with other people, often silently, and for a long time. After I learned this about myself, I was able to take responsibility for my own poor behaviours, and this helped me have better relationships with many people. Even now I sometimes fall back into these old patterns. But it is getting easier and easier to be aware of my actions and how they affect other people.

There are some people in my life who may never forgive me for some of the things I did. This used to tear me up inside. I used to obsess about how I have hurt certain people, and I strongly desired to make it right. These thoughts can still arise, and there a few people out there whom I know I hurt emotionally. But the reality is that this is in the past, and I am a different person today than when I was even a few years ago.

I have learned to forgive myself for many things I have done in the past. This includes not letting myself off the hook. Now I reflect on my poor behaviours and think about how I now have the capacity to do things differently.

I also have come to realise some of the things I did occurred when I was younger. These are the trials that we go through as we grow up and learn about ourselves. I still make mistakes with people and cross boundaries with them, but I like to think that I am more capable now of taking responsibility for my actions and learning from these experiences. Even now it sometimes takes me a while to learn my lessons; you just need to ask my wife. But I feel and know within myself that I am getting there.

Going back to my forgiveness process with my grandfather, an unexpected but awesome result of going through the process of forgiveness was getting in touch with my love. I found I was able to start fully experiencing self-love for the first time in a really long time. I was also able to start feeling the love that I shared with my grandfather and others in my life.

The lesson I learned much later around my forgiveness process with my grandfather was that of celebration. Only more recently was I able to realise that I could celebrate that I had forgiven him. He died a number of years ago, and I am glad that I was able to forgive him. It was my reflecting on this very thing that gave me cause to celebrate. When I celebrated this in my own, private way, it opened up a new path within me that let me feel not only more whole but also better able to give of myself to others in my life. After my celebration, I experienced a new depth of self-love and love to be shared with others.

When we embrace forgiveness within ourselves, extraordinary things can happen for us. For me, it was a transformative experience that opened up new things within and amazingly shifted relationships I had with others. In essence, what I experienced was the lifting of an emotional weight I had felt for years that had created patterns in my life. It was the opening up of love within me for myself and others, learning new ways to interact with those close to me, and learning to celebrate the good memories I had and the fact that I was able to shift and transform my thoughts and emotions.

Exercise

Think of something you have done that you find difficult to forgive yourself for. When you have done this, try the following; maybe even try to have fun with it as well if you can. Afterwards, you could also try to apply this to someone you want to forgive.

Think of it in terms of a past experience that is not in the present moment. Are these thoughts and feelings repetitive, and do they still serve you?

Now, I would like you to acknowledge and honour your emotions around this.

Has this experience affected your relationship with yourself or others?

Open yourself up to some self-love around this.

What does it feel like to say, "I forgive myself for this"?

Celebrate that you have been through a new process.

Chapter 10

Gratitude

I have learned that gratitude is an active process of accepting, appreciating, and acknowledging the abundant love that exists in others and myself.

Gratitude is a process that allows me to connect to my inner love, to express my personal power, and to nurture the relationships in my life.

What Brought Me to Gratitude

This is the chapter that almost did not happen but was actually meant to be. As I have been going through the process of finding my pathway to finishing this book, I realised that there were some changes that I needed to make beyond just doing an edit. Through much inner searching, many discussions with Libby, and a good, heartfelt discussion with my friend Nicola when she was visiting us here in Australia earlier in 2015, what I realised is that I needed to add more content. (By the way, Nicola has also written and published her own book, *Abigail's Rainbow*, about the loss of her daughter in a car accident and her own personal journey through bereavement. If you want some awesomeness in your life, get to know Nicola.)

I realised that the additional content was not just about adding to the chapters but also doing a restructuring of some of what I had already written and, of course, writing this chapter. All of this contributed to the anxiety over completing this book that I had been feeling. An anxiety about being seen in the world and revealing myself beyond my community work and my typical social media posts. So how did I work through this anxiety in relation to my writing, and what was some of my process I experienced in moving towards the completion of this piece of work?

To start with, I did not have a predefined process for working through my anxiety. I did, however, apply some of the processes I have discussed in this book along with other actions to support myself on this very personal journey.

As I mentioned already, I sought support from my wife, some friends, and from an accredited counsellor. Through seeking support from others, I was able to allow these relationships to assist me in moving through my anxiety. I also decided to honour this anxiety and give it the space it needed as opposed to how I used to often ignore this emotion and bury it inside of me. After I was able to acknowledge my anxiety, I could start to see some of the repetitive patterns I have in my life in relation to it. I also started to look at my anxiety from the present moment and remember that what has occurred in the past does not have to occur again.

One other thing I did that was helpful was book myself for a writing weekend away where I gave myself the time and freedom to explore my thoughts about finishing this book. What occurred to me on the writing weekend was that I needed to accept where I was at and be grateful for all the things in my life that had led me to where I was. This was a bit of an aha moment for me, and I realised that I needed to put a bit more of my own life into the book and acknowledge and write about acceptance and gratitude. Hence the beginning of this chapter was born. These things amongst others assisted me in starting to shift through my anxious state.

Something I would like to note is that when I was up to the point in my editing where I had decided to start writing this chapter, it was also the same week that I discovered that Dr. Wayne Dyer had died in his sleep. This initially made me sad as I have much respect for Dr. Dyer and his work of the past few years. His death, though, has also brought me into some love and happiness as it reminded me that I have much to be grateful for in my life. I may not have always agreed with everything that he said in his teachings, but he inspired me to reengage with my spiritual path at a time in my life when I was feeling really low and experiencing very dark thoughts about my existence. I am grateful to both Dr. Wayne Dyer and Louise Hay for their teachings. They both came into my life at just the right time and taught me about new levels of acceptance and gratitude, which is just exactly what I needed to find my inner inspiration to shift where I was at in my life a few years ago. This is all part of the path that led to this book, and it feels appropriate for me to acknowledge my gratitude to them now.

So What Is It?

So what is it about gratitude that is so important that I felt I should write about it? To start with, I have experienced and witnessed how gratitude can create change in the lives of others and in my life as well.

I have observed that when we practice gratitude, a few things can occur. Being grateful in the present moment can bring on a sense of peacefulness. When someone expresses gratitude towards me for something I have done, this can lift my spirits and make me feel better. In close relationships, gratitude is also a way for me to share my love with others. I have experienced this bringing me closer to those I have expressed this to.

When I look at things such as these, I see that for me, gratitude is a process that allows me to own my personal power and share my love. I feel powerful with gratitude as it is something that I do in the present moment. It can be expressed without judgement, and it can potentially turn challenging situations with others into positive experiences. I feel gratitude is also a part of the language of love that we can all speak. When I start to think about gratitude and examine it more closely from my personal perspective, I see that what I am doing when I am expressing gratitude is really an act of sharing my love.

I see gratitude as a process, and part of this involves it being active. By this I mean it takes an active choice and action by me to engage in being grateful. When I do this, it becomes experiential for me. In practical terms, this can be shown when I have had experiences of gratitude such as when I say thank you to the worker at a store who assisted me, being thankful to my friends who supported me through hard times, and so on.

In essence, I am also saying that it takes another for me to be able to experience gratitude that is either received or given. I have learned that it can be a powerful connecting element for me in my life.

Gratitude can also be an opportunity for me to learn much about life in general and myself. I have had experiences when I have been grateful to someone, and he or she has not acknowledged the gratitude. I have also had times when I expected to receive gratitude from others for things I have done, and it was not given to me. In both scenarios, I have learned that I am attached to an expectation of what I think others' reactions should be when we all know is that life does not always work that way. I am learning that when I act in this way, I am not actually being truly grateful as I am engaging in judgement. This I struggle with sometimes. I often expect people to be grateful, and when they are not, I get upset or disappointed. I am slowly learning how to engage in gratitude in an unconditional manner. It is taking me practice, and thus, it is much like how I am learning to bring unconditional love into my life.

When I remember to be unconditionally grateful and loving in my life, I am much more relaxed and accepting of the situations I am experiencing. It takes practice, and my anxious mind can be slow to shift its ways. But I know from experience that it is not impossible to do this, and that makes me hopeful for myself.

According to the *Online Oxford Dictionary,* the standard definition of "gratitude" is, "The quality of being thankful; readiness to show appreciation for and to return kindness."[19] Most of us know this definition even if we do not use these exact words. However, I do like the idea of being thankful, and have seen it referred to as an important thing in many spiritual, religious, and cultural contexts. I have come across teachings about thankfulness/gratitude in things I have read about Christianity, Islam, Judaism, Buddhism, Hinduism, and nonsecular spiritual teachings. Even when I used to consider myself an atheist, I was thankful for things in my life. For example, I was thankful to my parents and brother for loving me and supporting me through the difficult times in my life.

I also think that it is an awesome idea that gratitude can be about returning of a kindness. There is something about this that seems right to me. It feels to me like an act of sharing and meeting. When I reflect on times when I have returned a kindness to someone or engaged in kindness on someone else's behalf, I remember feeling really good at that time. It is almost as though the act of sharing or returning a kindness opens up a direct link to my heart and the love that is held within in it.

The Four A's

What I want to do now is expand a bit more upon my personal sense of what gratitude is. I already mentioned how, for me, gratitude is an expression of love. Now I want to view gratitude through the lens of what I have just recently thought of as the four A's: acceptance, appreciation, acknowledgement, and abundance.

When I think of gratitude, I also think of acceptance. To me, all acts of gratitude start with accepting that the circumstances are what they are in the moment. Through the act of accepting the situation that I am in, I am able to tap into my personal power. Through the act of acceptance, I can start to ground myself in the present moment where my power truly lies.

Part of the act of acceptance is coming to peace with the thoughts and emotions that arise when I am in a situation where I cannot change the circumstances. No amount of desire or wishful thinking can change the experiences that have led to any present moment situation. This desire for things to be different can cause much emotional and intellectual anguish. For me, learning to accept is a part of the process of learning to relax, practicing my inner peace, and opening myself to the love that exists within me.

I have discovered that learning to accept is also about recognising my own inner power. The power I have to make a difference in my life and in the lives of others. It is about learning to accept who I am no matter what has happened and what I have done. The process of acceptance has taught me that when I am in resistance, I am not necessarily accepting the situation I am in. When I start to recognise my resistance, this can point me in the direction of what it is I may need to accept and honour in my life.

The next part of gratitude is learning to appreciate what it is that I have accepted. This is a process of starting to attach some deeper, love-based emotional connection to gratitude. I can sometimes accept things without a lot of emotional connection, but to appreciate something, I am starting to engage in an act of learning to more fully understand it and assign some positive personal value to it. When I accept something, I am engaging in an internal process of attempting to perceive as much of the situation as my awareness is able to so that I can discern the value of it relative to what I am doing.

Within the process of appreciating something, I start to find a pathway to being grateful for the experiences I have had. When I find myself able to be grateful for these experiences, including ones I have considered to be horrible, I am on the path of learning to share and express my love more fully. Being grateful for "bad" things can be difficult, and I explore this a little a bit further into the chapter.

For me, accepting and appreciating are very much internal processes. Even though appreciation and acknowledgement are often seen as synonymous with each other for the purposes of what I am conveying here, there is a distinction that exists within my own mind with the way that I use these words. To my mind, appreciation is more of an internal process of feeling and assessing, whereas acknowledging is the act of opening up and reaching out to others to let them know that I have accepted what has happened and am in appreciation of it as well.

The act of acknowledgement is an action whereby I am actively showing what it is that I am in appreciation of. In other words, it takes what I am experiencing internally and makes it external, thus becoming an action that can be observed. As gratitude is not a solitary thing, I feel that it is the act of acknowledgement that sets it truly into action.

Acknowledgement is an outward expression of love and appreciation. It takes the internal experience of gratitude and shifts it into a relational one. Acknowledgement turns gratitude into action. With acknowledgement we open up our love to be shared with others.

The last A in this list is abundance. You may be wondering what abundance has to do with being grateful. When I am in a loving mindset, I can see abundance surrounding me in my life. I am not talking just about a material abundance I have accumulated. I am also talking about the abundance of beauty I see in life, the abundance of emotions I have to experience, an abundance of people to interact with, and an abundance of opportunities that I have to experience and learn from.

As I see gratitude being linked to love, I also see it as being potentially infinite like love. When I am truly being grateful, it is without boundaries, limits, or judgements, much like love. So as I see gratitude as something that can exist without limit, I also see it as being abundant. It is almost like gratitude and abundance are two sides of the same coin called love. This may seem kind of strange, but when I am expressing gratitude, I am sharing an abundance of love. At the same time, I am expressing gratitude for the abundance I see and experience in my life.

Eckhart Tolle, in an interview with Oprah Winfrey, said, "to see the abundance that surrounds you, even if you're very poor in the eyes of the world, the abundance is always there around you, but you need to recognize it, acknowledge it. And another word for that is gratitude."[20]

After we engage in acceptance, appreciation, and acknowledgement, and create the circumstances for gratitude to become active with opening up our love to be shared, we can then experience abundance. What I mean is that not only am I opening myself up to share love but with abundance, I also open myself up to connecting with the love that exists within others. I have observed that as I empower myself to recognise abundance, it makes it easier for abundance to flow towards me as I am both readier and more willing to receive it. Think of it like how we may experience love in our lives. If we are experiencing our inner love, it is easier for us to see it all around us. It is also easier for us to experience it in return from others. People are often more easily able to share love with others who are already in a loving mindset, and this, to me, is much like abundance.

You're Talking Crap

Maybe you are wondering how we can be grateful for crap things in our lives. How can we be thankful for horrible and distressing stuff that happens to those we care about or to us?

Well, of course, this cannot be easy at times. But it can get easier with practice. I really have struggled with these types of thoughts in my life quite regularly. My ego always wants me to be right, and I often jump onto my own self-righteous bandwagon and do not want to see the role I play in my own unpleasant experiences. Then there are those times when things happened to me that I had no control over at the time, and I felt sorry for myself or even played the martyr about it, allowing myself to live in these past experiences. Learning to be grateful for horrible experiences can definitely be a hard thing for me to swallow and accept.

I have learned that accepting these things can be powerful for me as they teach me to self-reflect on my actions and reactions. It has taught me that these experiences can be learning ones that give me knowledge about how I move through the world and engage with other people. Much like how the car accident that almost took my life has now become an awesome experience that I have learned much from.

I have already discussed how to shift this kind of thinking, but I think it is worthwhile to briefly mention here again as it is a struggle I have had and something that I have also observed others struggling with. I have learned how powerful reframing my experiences can be and how this has led to personal healing and learning.

In the most extreme examples of this, what comes to mind right now are acts of extreme violence perpetrated against others. I admit that linking gratitude to stuff like this is very difficult. For me, life gratitude and forgiveness have been two significant ingredients in my personal reconciliation recipe. They provide me with part of the framework that has allowed me to shift away from being stuck in the past with unhelpful thoughts and feelings.

Let me use a personal example of how I have recently started to use these processes to think a little bit differently about such a large event as World War 2, for example. I recently realised that I have more to be grateful for beyond the tide that was turned against fascism. I can also be grateful that there was some learning internationally that came from World War 2. As we all know, many atrocities were committed in this war. Now, I want to be clear here in saying that I do not think that these horrors were justifications for what I am saying, but as a result of what occurred, some things to be grateful for have come about. In particular, I am thinking of the Declaration of Human Rights.

I know these rights are currently ignored by many individuals and governments around the world, and sometimes, the international structures that have been set up to enshrine these rights can be ineffective in the face of politics and violence. However, when I read the declaration, I see a great document that can be a basis for human interaction that is respectful. It provides us with a great guide for how we treat each other in the world and can sometimes guide us towards avoiding or stopping atrocities. I think that this declaration is something that I can definitely be grateful for, and it is also something that came about as the result of the many awful things that happened in World War 2.

I now want to link gratitude a bit more to being awesome. To me, there is a fifth A involved with gratitude, and this is awe. Early on I referred to how part of being awesome is to be in awe of something. As a reminder, the official definitions contain words like "reverential respect," "fear," "wonder," "veneration," "sacred," "sublime," "remarkable," and "impressive." All these words apply to things we can be grateful for as well. If I am in awe of something, I can also be grateful for it as it can provide me with opportunities for learning and love. So as we encounter things that we previously have labelled as "bad," we can learn to be grateful for the opportunities they can provide. This is another way to reconcile my thoughts around horrible experiences and events. These events, like my car accident or even historical things like World War 2, are definitely things for me to hold in awe. Because I can do this, I know I can eventually find learning from them to be grateful for.

Another thing I would like to briefly mention in relation to gratitude being awesome are the feelings I get when I am grateful for something. When I have been truly grateful for something, this can often make me feel larger than life and connected to what I have shown my appreciation and thankfulness for. Also, when I am the recipient of gratitude, this can feel awesome as well as making me feel loved and appreciated. How awesome is it when someone says thank you and means it, or he or she lets you know that they are grateful for something you have done? How else can I describe it but saying it is awesome? In particular, the awe in the awesome can come forward when these things come from unexpected sources such as a stranger, someone you have little contact with, or even someone you may have had conflict with before. Gratitude can be humbling, not in a shameful way, but in a way that connects us to our hearts and the goodness we can all feel in our lives.

The Spiritual

Throughout this book I have not referred too much to the spiritual if at all directly. In the case of gratitude, I want to speak about it in relation to my own spirituality. My spirituality is an awesome part of my life, and even when I considered myself atheist, I considered myself spiritual. One of the reasons for this was that I was in gratitude for what I had in my life, such as the people I cared about and having good food and homes to live in. At that time, I was also vegetarian, and this was a part of my spiritual practice.

For me, gratitude is still a spiritual practice, and this has many connotations when I think about it. To start with, I have already referred to how I see gratitude as being connected to love. This is part of the foundation for considering the spiritual connection. As I am grateful, I connect with the love that exists within me and, at the same time, open myself to share this love with the love that exists within others.

When I view gratitude from this perspective, I see how it opens me up to both experiencing and accepting some of the paradoxes that I have observed for my life. In particular, I am thinking about the paradox of having my own awareness of self while also knowing that on some levels, I am indivisible from others. In my life I have had both experiences of my self and experiences where I have felt and observed my indivisibility from others.

When I am grateful, I am connecting to the love that exists within. As I do this, I am connecting with a conception of myself as a whole and separate entity. In some ways, I could say it is my whole self—my personal identity—that is in gratitude for what I am thankful for. But then as I engage in the act of being grateful, I am opening myself up to connecting with others. As I do this, I can connect with the love that exists within others. In that way, I think this love is universal as within all of us. Then, as I connect with others, I start to experience the universality of love and the abundance that it represents. If we all have love within us, we are all connected and indivisible.

So to me this is the paradox. I have an experience of self where I feel grateful and then as I express it, I come into connection with others through our innate love and can then experience this indivisible aspect of life. From my perspective, we are all expressions of love and can open ourselves up to sharing through gratitude. Then as we do this, we can feel and experience our indivisible connection with others.

Another way that I think about this is that gratitude is where self-actualisation meets what I call we-actualisation. To me, self-actualisation arises as I engage in the process of being grateful for something without strings attached or judgement. As I enter into a space of nonjudgement, I come into connection with my inner love and the arising desire to share this with someone else. In essence, I am actualising my love in this process and transforming it into something that can be experiential. To my way of thinking, I am actualising an internal experience.

So what do I mean by we-actualisation? To me, this is a natural progression from self-actualisation. It is part of the process of experiencing the paradox I outlined previously. The we part is when I have an experience of indivisibility with the other. In spiritual terms, it is part of the path of becoming enlightened. I have not just an understanding that I am connected to the other but also an experience of it as well.

There is a natural progression here. When I start to actualise myself, this starts me on a path of realising that the self in some ways is an illusion and that I am actually part of the larger entity of life itself. As the self starts to dissipate, I start to realise, and I have even had very brief moments of experiencing the indivisibility of life. To me, this is the we-actualisation. So at the same time, I can have an experience of self and an experience of an ultimate we.

Now, getting back to gratitude. As I am going through the process of expressing my thankfulness to the other, this allows me to be open to sharing love, which I have mentioned a number times now. It is this opening to our love that creates the experience of being able to perceive both the self and the we. Gratitude melts the barriers that exist between others and myself and lets me see that our love is naturally connected and is, in fact, a part of the same universal love that we all hold within ourselves.

As part of my spiritual practice, I also see that gratitude can be a healing process for me. In particular, when I think of it in relation to my processes of forgiveness. One of the most powerful things I have ever experienced has been taking forgiveness to what I now think of as the next stage. This next stage is all about not just forgiving from a place of nonjudgmental love but learning to genuinely be grateful for the experience as well. In my estimation learning to be grateful for the crap in my life is one of the most empowering things I can do.

This is a truly powerful experience in my life. This is one of the ways that I can ultimately take control of my life. I am not going to say it is easy. I do get caught up in my thinking and easily fall into martyrdom and "poor me" thinking. I did this around my car accident, I sometimes do this in relationships, and I also do this in relation to jobs I have held to name a few quick examples of how I engage in this behaviour.

The more I practice the connection between gratitude and forgiveness, though, the more powerful I feel. The process often is that I go through my poor me thoughts, sometimes for a long time, but when I remember how I want to be, the internal shift can start to occur. As I have mentioned, I can get anxious. When I am in this state, my mind can race. It can take me a while—sometimes days, weeks, and months—before my perspective on a particular experience starts to shift.

This shift is the healing process I am now referring to. As I shift my thoughts and emotions around something I have labelled as not so good, a healing takes place within me. I feel lighter, my tension decreases, and I can think more clearly. I actually start to feel healed in relation to the experience that I have had. I would like to note, though, that for some experiences—for example those that are traumatic or involve grief—it is not a linear path. So just because I feel healed does not mean that the negative emotions and thoughts will not come back. However, what this does mean for me is that when they do recur, and they do, it gets easier and easier over time for me to work through these things.

The Other Seven Practices

Now I speak briefly about gratitude in relation to the other practices, much like I did in the chapter on forgiveness.

To begin with, when I think about gratitude and how it relates to being in the present moment, it helps me to remember that gratitude is in itself something that occurs in the now. It is a present moment process. When I am being grateful, I am honouring what I am experiencing in the present moment.

Part of this, to me, is that not only am I acknowledging and honouring a present moment experience, I am also honouring life as a whole. I only ever truly experience life in the present moment, and when I show gratitude for something, I am also showing my love for life. When I am being grateful for a past experience, I am also honouring it in the present moment and connecting it to the personal power I have through engaging in present moment awareness. These are ways for me to shift how I think and feel about past experiences.

In regards to the future and gratitude, what occurs to me is that if I am in a mindset of believing that my future experiences are things to be grateful for, then as I have new experiences in the now, I am already setting myself up to engage in them from a perspective of love. Through doing this, I understand how this can be helpful for me.

This has been a recent revelation for me. As I enter experiences feeling like I can already be grateful for them, the likelihood of me embracing the experience as one that will serve me increases. If I see every experience as something that I can be grateful for, I am tapping into the abundance of life and love that surrounds me. I may often forget to have this type of present moment thinking, and that is okay as so much in my life takes practice. What I am now aware of, however, is that when I can remember to be grateful for whatever experiences I am encountering, I can have a more powerful present moment awareness with the potential to shift any emotions or thinking that may arise out of habit and no longer serve me.

As I learn to be grateful for all my emotions, I am again learning to be grateful for myself. I can be grateful for emotions as they can teach me about myself, let me discover my boundaries, and provide me with many opportunities for learning. In the chapter on emotions, I talked about honouring the full range of emotions that we all experience. To me, gratitude is a way of honouring all the things in my life, and this, of course, includes my emotions. I have learned to be grateful for the emotions that I have. It is my emotions that connect me to my experiences. If I am honouring my emotions, I am actually expressing gratitude for them.

As I discussed in my chapter on repetitive behaviours, I can reframe how I think about behaviours that I have labelled as "bad habits." I talked about how our behaviours can sometimes be creative ways to assist us through difficult and challenging situations. I would like to suggest that adding gratitude to the process of honouring these behaviours is a way of assisting with shifting how we can think about them. I can be grateful for these so-called bad behaviours because at one point they served me. When I am doing this, I am honouring and being grateful to myself for creatively navigating my way through my life.

When I am being grateful for my repetitive behaviours, I am also being grateful for the learning I have gained from them. As I mentioned earlier, my behaviours can act as awesome signposts, bringing me into awareness of how I can respond to situations as opposed to reacting to them. I am grateful that through this I am learning how to better express myself in ways that serve who and what I want to be in my life and the world.

My next chapters were about relationships and love. As I have already spoken about this, I will only say a few more words. I just want to reiterate that gratitude can strengthen relationships. As I accept and honour myself and others, both mutual respect and a sharing of love have the potential to occur. It is awesome to be able to both receive and express gratitude as it is the great connector in my estimation.

Now in relation to celebration, I feel that gratitude forms a big part of it. Essentially, when I am celebrating anything, I am being grateful for it. If I am celebrating something that is in relation to me, I am honouring and expressing gratitude towards myself for what I have achieved. When I am celebrating the achievements of others, not only am I honouring them, but I am also showing them through my words, actions, and emotions that I am grateful for them as well.

I have already referred to gratitude and forgiveness and how when I put gratitude into the mix of forgiveness, an awesome new depth or height of forgiveness can occur. I will just mention here that forgiveness combined with gratitude not only connects us more fully to others but also acknowledges others and ourselves. At the same time, it reminds us that upon reflection of past experiences, we can choose emotional reactions that better serve us.

Chapter 11

Pulling It Together and Summing It Up

I would like to start this final chapter by having you think again about some of the first questions I posed at the beginning of the book. Think about the following as you go through these. When you are answering these questions, do you notice any differences or shifts in how you think about your answers compared to when you answered them at the beginning of the book? Maybe the answers are the same, but you may have a slightly different focus or take on them than you did originally.

Again there are no right or wrong answers. What I am really doing is encouraging you to reflect on your thoughts regardless of whether you agree with what I have shared. Okay, let's get started.

Exercise

Please write down three awesome things about yourself.

Please write down three awesome things about relationships in your life.

Please write down three awesome things about your community.

Please write down three things you would like to be awesome in your life.

What Is Change?

Throughout this book I have written about processes involving change, so I thought that I would share some of what change is for me. Of course, change happens all the time, and as the saying goes, "Change is the only constant."[21] For the purpose of what I have written, though, I am talking about change as something that we can actively engage in; those things that are within our control to have an influence over.

Change in the context of what I have written is the process of shifting our routine processes of emotions, thoughts, and actions in ways that serve us better in expressing who we want to be. Change occurs when we start to think about things in a different way, when we start to have different emotional reactions, and when we engage in different actions than what we usually do. Change to me is not always about epiphanies or huge aha moments where the figurative light bulb above our head switches on. It can be those things, of course, but to me, it is also about regular, everyday things. Part of the change process could be as straightforward as drinking an extra glass of water each day as I have realised that this can assist me with staying more hydrated.

Another aspect of change could be a slight shift in thinking where we do not actually change any behaviour at all. We just allow ourselves to see what we are doing in a new light, to acknowledge and honour the variety of things that we experience and are in our lives.

I am sure you have probably heard of the idea of the self-fulfilling prophecy, where when we believe that something is going to happen and then it does, people associate this with others and or negative things. For example, I have seen how when I or others wake up and think it will be a bad day, it will often end up being a bad day for us. We carry this unhelpful thought with us for the whole day and allow it to taint our interpretation of everything we encounter. Now, sometimes a bad thing does happen to us that can be out of our control, of course, but I am referring to the types of things where we do have influence. For example, I may go into a meeting grumpy, and that may trigger other people being grumpy back with me. I can have control and choice over that sort of situation and enter into it in a more open and accepting matter and have a better meeting as a result.

What I suggest is that we take control of this type of thinking and, using our awareness and practicing different techniques in the way that we approach our lives, start to do things like saying, "Today is going to be an awesome day," instead of waking up and thinking, *Damn, not another bloody day to contend with.*

When we start living from the moment and creating positive thoughts and actions, we begin to manifest more helpful realities for ourselves. When we choose to be happy and stay happy, we are manifesting happy. Now remember, I am not saying that we live in a realm of complete positivity; far from it. What I am suggesting is that through this process, we can learn to engage in all our emotions and start to choose the appropriate mental and emotional reactions for circumstances that serve us the best. It is okay to be angry, frustrated, or sad as these emotions can serve us well. I have, however, experienced how if I go through my day with love and compassion, I have a better day than when I stay in a bad mood.

Part of being awesome is recognising that I have the power to change my attitudes and life through choosing and honouring the thoughts and actions that I engage in. Of course, this might take practice, but for me this has been a wonderful path to follow as it has helped me immensely. Through practicing and actively engaging in the types of thoughts and actions I have talked about in this book, I have learned that I can create changes in my life that serve me in ways that are much more productive and healthy than what I used to believe.

My awesomeness exists within me and can show itself on a daily basis if I allow myself to get in touch with it. I can share it with other people and take it with me wherever I go. My awesomeness allows me to get in touch with all the wonderful experiences of thought, emotion, and connection I have within myself and with those around me. My awesomeness allows me to experience the complete fullness of my being and gives me the opportunity to share this with others, thus leading me to an extraordinary life.

A Quick Review of the Insights

I now just want to briefly go over each of my practices in a miniature review and quickly share how each one has had an impact on my life.

With my first insightful practice on learning to live from the present moment, I have personally learned that change can happen through simple and straightforward things such as learning to develop awareness of the world around me and of my own thoughts and emotions. Part of this has been accomplished through just reminding myself that I only ever truly live my life in the present moment. When I remember to say this to myself regularly, I feel I am much more in control of circumstances I can make decisions about.

In Alcoholics and Narcotics Anonymous groups, some people adopt the serenity prayer written by Reinhold Niebuhr. If you have a different belief system, you can do something like alter the following prayer into an affirmation where you appeal to your inner self to assist. This is a good way of looking at how we can make choices in our lives.

> God, grant me the serenity to accept the
> things I cannot change,
> The courage to change the things I can,
> And wisdom to know the difference.

In the second practice, I learned that I could create change through acknowledging and honouring my repetitive behaviours. I have learned that habits that I thought were bad were actually helpful behaviours to me when they started. I have seen that when I start to recognise them as such, I can make clearer choices around my behaviours, creating ones that serve me better. One way I have done this is through simply doing things such as saying something to myself like, "My habits are not the completely horrible things that I thought they were," and, "This behaviour was something that once served but no longer does so now." Remembering that when I say these things that it is okay to have had the negative thoughts, and I can cut myself some slack if the old repetitive patterns reemerge. Some of them have been around for a long time, after all, and I need practice in making new choices for myself.

For my third practice, I have seen how honouring all of my emotions is important to me. When I honour all of my emotions and give them the space they deserve in my life, I can learn more about myself. The simple way for me to do this has been to do something like saying to myself, "It is okay and natural for me to have had that feeling, and I do not need to feel guilty for experiencing it," or, "This emotion has helped me to learn …" I have gained the knowledge that all my emotions are a part of me, and to deny them is to deny parts of who I am.

With practice of the fourth, I have seen how building a healthy relationship with myself assists me with having better relationships with others. Also, when I spend time building relationships with others, it helps me to achieve awesome things that I would not be able to do on my own. A good example of building a relationship with myself has been in making small lifestyle changes that, over time, have positively affected my health, such as walking an extra twenty to thirty minutes on most days. In regards to other people, it has been as simple as taking the time to catch up with them more often and mutually sharing how our lives have been.

In practice number five I have learned that loving myself is a direct route to my awesome inner self. When I love myself, I am also more compassionate with myself for the mistakes I make in my life. When I do this, it is much easier for me to extend this love to other people as well, learning that expressing love to others is also a way of expressing self-love at the same time. One easy thing I have done in this area of my life is to have a note posted to the mirror in my home that says, "I love you, life loves you, and I love life."

Through my sixth practice I discovered that celebration is a way to honour my self-achievements and the achievements of others while also giving me opportunities to express love and be creative. In regards to myself, an easy thing I have done to help me remember the importance of celebration is to mark even small achievements in my life. A good example for me was when I took my wife out for dinner after I had achieved the development of the outline for this book. Another example has been to buy my wife some flowers when she completed a challenging piece of work for her business.

With the seventh practice, I learned that through self-forgiveness, I can be compassionate and loving to myself and to others. It is when I have experienced self-forgiveness that I can share this with others, giving me the opportunity to share my love as well. To me, a straightforward way to support this process has been to remember that the experience where I felt I was hurt was in the past, and I do not need to remain hurt in the present, thus freeing myself from inhibitive thoughts and emotions. This, along with reminding myself that there is a lesson to learn from the incident about my inner strength and resilience, has been very powerful for me.

Finally, with the eighth and last practice I have learned how gratitude is an active process of accepting, appreciating, and acknowledging the abundant love that exists in others and myself. It is a process that allows me to connect to my inner love, to express my personal power, and to nurture the relationships in my life. I have also learned how gratitude can be very much a part of my own spiritual practices, allowing me to be in service to both others and myself.

In Conclusion

As a whole, when I look at all of my insights, I see how they can all work together to support each other in assisting me to realise that I have an awesome life. Each one on its own can do this and provide me with insight and an avenue to experiencing and acknowledging how I can live an extraordinary life. They can also all work together to assist me with creating shifts and changes in my life that go towards serving the healthy version of who I want to be. These insights help me to realise that being awesome is something that already exists within me and that I can tap into it at any time.

I am a work in progress as I am changing all the time. I am still learning about others and myself, and as I gain new insights, I learn more and more how to implement them into my life. I am still practising and working on a lot of what I have shared with you. I have, however, begun to realise that I am an awesome piece of work in the process of realising that I am perfect as who I am with all the emotions, thoughts, and experiences that I have had, am having, and will have.

I would like to leave you with two last things to take away with you.

Clear, Claim, and Create

This last tool I am giving you is much like the stop, swap, and send I taught you about earlier in the book. It is simple to use and has assisted me with difficult and challenging situations. I call it clear, claim, and create. It is a process I use for quickly clearing my mind, claiming my power, and creating my reality.

It simply goes like this. When I am in a situation that feels overwhelming or I am having difficulty with a challenge, I first say to myself the words clear, claim, and create. I then clear my mind for a moment of the stressful thoughts that I have been having. After I have cleared my mind, I will say to myself, "Claim my power." This reminds me that my true power exists in the present moment and I have an opportunity to respond to instead of react to, the situation. Then I can create in my mind a scenario about how this situation can be different for me.

Clear, claim, and create is simple, and it works for me. It slows down my racing thoughts and then reminds me that I can choose a different reaction or response if that is what works best in the situation. Finally, I can potentially be creative in making the next choice necessary in the current situation. Through this I am building and using my awareness and recognising that I may be in a repetitive pattern or emotion, and allowing myself the space to choose whether to honour my current thoughts and emotions or to choose others that may be appropriate in the situation for me.

Now It Is Awesome Intention Time

My Final Exercise

Take some time now to write out what your next awesome intention will be that will assist you in leading your extraordinary life. It can be big or small. Remember to make it about living from the present moment. Let it come from love, and like we did in an earlier exercise, set a practice for it so that it becomes a reality for you.

My Final Thought for You

Awesomeness, like love and happiness, is something that all of us already have within us. It is my hope that my words will not necessarily set you on a path to leading an extraordinary life but help you to realise that you are already awesome.

At the beginning of the book I made a joke about thanking you for buying the book. This was meant to be humorous, but I am stripping back the humour here, and now with my heart, I am thanking you for buying the book and taking the time to read it.

In Gratitude,
Sebastian King

manifestAwesome@gmail.com.au
www.manifestAwesome@wordpress.com

Endnotes

1 Lau-tzu. *Tao Te Ching*. Trans. Stephen Mitchell (London: Kyle Books, 2011), p. 33.

2 Oxford Dictionaries. 2015. http://www.oxforddictionaries.com/definition/english/awe.

3 Merriam-Webster. 2015. http://www.merriam-webster.com/dictionary/awe.

4 Oxford Dictionaries. 2015. http://www.oxforddictionaries.com/definition/english/Extraordinary.

5 Merriam-Webster. 2015. http://www.merriam-webster.com/dictionary/Extraordinary.

6 1. Abraham H. Maslow, *A Theory of Human Motivation*. eBook edition (Start Publishing LLC, 2012).; Abraham H. Maslow, *Motivation and Personality*. 3rd ed. (New York: Harper & Row Publishers, 1970).

7 Lau-tzu, *Tao Te Ching*. Trans. Stephen Mitchell (London: Kyle Books, 2011), p. 33.

8   Viktor E. Frankl, *Man's Search for Meaning.* (St. Ives plc, Great Britain: Rider, 2008).

9   Wayne Dyer, "The Power of I Am." 2012. < http://www.drwaynedyer.com/blog/the-power-of-i-am/.

10 Sri Ramanasramam, *The Teachings of Bhagavan Sri Ramana Maharshi* (Tiruvannamalai, S. India: V. S. Ramanan, 1999).

11 *Vipassana Meditation.* "Mr. S. N. Goenka Background." https://www.dhamma.org/en/about/goenka.

12 Christopher Titmuss. http://www.christophertitmuss.org.

13 Frederick S. Perls, Ralph F. Hefferline, and Paul Goodman, Paul. *Gestalt Therapy: Excitement and Growth in the Human Condition* (Reading, Berkshire: Souvenir Press, 2006), pp. 400–428.

14 Edwin C. Nevis, *Gestalt Therapy: Perspectives and Applications.* (Cambridge, MA: Gestalt Press, 2000), pp. 27–29.

15 Gary M. Yontef and Reinhard Fuhr, "Gestalt Therapy: Theory of Change." *Gestalt Therapy: History, Theory, and Practice.* Ansel L. Woldt and Sarah M. Toman (eds.) (Thousand Oaks, California: Sage Publications, 2005), pp. 85–86.

16 Brené Brown, *Shame v. Guilt,* January 14, 2013. http://brenebrown.com/2013/01/14/2013114shame-v-guilt-html.

17 CultureSynch. *Tribal Leadership Book.* 2012. http://www.triballeadership.net.

18 Abraham H. Maslow, *Motivation and Personality,* 3rd ed, (New York: Harper & Row Publishers, 1970), pp. 278–279.

19 Oxford Dictionaries. 2015. http://www.oxforddictionaries.com/definition/english/gratitude.

20 *Oprah.com.* "Master Class Transcript. A New Earth Online Course." 2008. http://images.oprah.com/images/obc_classic/book/2008/anewearth/ane_chapter7_transcript.pdf.

21 "Heraclitus: Life Is Flux," *The Online Ancient History Encyclopedia,* 2012. This explains how the pre-Socratic philosopher Heraclitus of Ephesus inspired the quote, "Change is the only constant." http://www.ancient.eu/article/183/.

Printed in the United States
By Bookmasters